BECOMING *a* HOUSE *of* PRAYER

ERIC CÉLÉRIER

BECOMING *a* HOUSE *of* PRAYER

A 30-DAY DEVOTIONAL TO CARRY GOD'S PRESENCE INTO EVERY AREA OF YOUR LIFE

DAVID C COOK
transforming lives together

BECOMING A HOUSE OF PRAYER
Published by David C Cook
4050 Lee Vance Drive
Colorado Springs, CO 80918 U.S.A.

Integrity Music Limited, a Division of David C Cook
Brighton, East Sussex BN1 2RE, England

Library of Congress Control Number 2025938524
ISBN 978-0-8307-9103-3
eISBN 978-0-8307-9104-0

This edition is an English adaptation based on the original French work
Devenez une Maison de Prière: Les mystères cachés du Notre Père
© 2024 Eric Célérier. Published in France. ISBN 978-2-9594752-0-7
This translation was generated with the assistance of ChatGPT-4.

The Team: Michael Covington, Luke McKinnon, Stephanie
Bennett, Judy Gillispie, Susan Murdock
Cover Design: Leah Von Fange

Printed in the United States of America
First English Edition 2025

1 2 3 4 5 6 7 8 9 10

073025

Our Father in heaven,
hallowed be your name.
your kingdom come,
your will be done,
on earth as it is in heaven.
Give us today our daily bread.
And forgive us our debts,
as we also have forgiven our debtors.
And lead us not into temptation,
but deliver us from the evil one,
for yours is the kingdom and the
power and the glory forever.
Amen!

—Jesus Christ

What People Say about the Lord's Prayer

"Using the Lord's Prayer as a floor plan, take a tour of the home God intended for you. Warm your heart by the fire in the living room. Nourish your spirit in the kitchen. Seek fellowship in the family room. Step into the hallway and find forgiveness."

—Max Lucado

"The prayer of the Our Father is 'truly the summary of the whole gospel.'"

—Tertullian

"The Lord's Prayer is the most perfect of prayers.... In it we ask, not only for all the things we can rightly desire, but also in the sequence they should be desired."

—Thomas Aquinas

"The Our Father is the most excellent prayer because it is the work of the Son of God, who showed us how we should pray and what we should ask for."

—Francis de Sales

"Since our Lord is the author of this prayer, it is without a doubt the most sublime, the loftiest, and the most excellent."

—Martin Luther

CONTENTS

Welcome to *Becoming a House of Prayer*

Dear friend,

I'm so glad you're here. It's a real joy—and a great honor—to walk this journey with you.

This isn't just a book you're holding; it's an invitation. An invitation to go deeper than you may have ever gone before. To step inside the house of prayer Jesus built with His own words—the Our Father—and discover room after room filled with beauty, truth, and life.

Think of this as a spiritual pilgrimage.

I encourage you: don't rush.

Take it slow.

Savor one chapter a day. Let each phrase of the Lord's Prayer become part of you, shaping how you see God, yourself, and the world around you.

When Jesus said, "This, then, is how you should pray ..." (Matt. 6:9), He wasn't giving us a formula—He was giving us a way to live.

The book is divided into thirty short chapters—easy to read in just a few minutes each. But don't let the simplicity fool you; each chapter holds treasures you can only discover by lingering, listening, opening your heart wide.

Inside you'll also find real testimonies from men and women who walked the journey through this book before you—stories born from real life, real struggle, and real breakthroughs. They're here to remind you that you're not alone.

At the end of each chapter, you'll find a prayer—not to memorize but to inspire your own conversation with the Father. Feel free to adapt these prayers, stretch them, cry them out, whisper them in the quiet. Make them yours.

My deepest prayer is that this book wouldn't just change your prayer life—it would change your whole life.

That you would discover you are not just invited to pray but you are invited to **become a house of prayer** yourself.

A place where heaven meets earth.

A place where the Father loves to dwell.

I'll be walking with you, chapter by chapter, day by day. I'm praying for you already.

Let's begin.

With love and hope,
Your brother and friend,
Eric Célérier

Who Am I?

My name is Eric Célérier, and my passion is simple yet profound: to bridge technology and theology to help people encounter the love of Jesus in real, transformative ways.

For the past thirty-four years, my wife, Muriel, has been my faithful companion—both in life and ministry. Together, we've raised three amazing children and now have the immense joy of being grandparents. Our journey has been woven with unity, grace, and a shared mission: to make God's love visible in a broken world.

In 2006, I founded **Jesus.net**, a global movement now bringing together over 130 ministries across the world, dedicated to digital evangelism and discipleship. Today, I'm also leading a new adventure: **HelloBible.app**—the world's first intelligent biblical assistant, designed to help people engage with Scripture through the power of AI, while keeping the heart firmly centered on Jesus.

Throughout the years, God has given me the honor of mentoring leaders, advising ministries, and speaking into the lives of people across the globe. As a global ambassador for *The Chosen* I've seen firsthand how storytelling can open hearts to the gospel. I also continue to serve ministries by helping them navigate the opportunities of the digital age with strategy, prayer, and innovation.

As an author, my writings are born from this same longing: to help people encounter God personally, meaningfully, every day.

This book, *Becoming a House of Prayer*, is especially close to my heart.

It's not just a study of the Lord's Prayer—it's an invitation to live it, breathe it, and build your life around it. My prayer is that through these reflections, you will experience God's presence so deeply that your entire life becomes a house where heaven touches earth.

No matter the project—whether it's launching innovative apps, writing devotionals, mentoring leaders, or simply sharing a coffee with a friend—one thing drives me:

To inspire you to walk closely with God, and to experience His love, His truth, and His beauty in ways that change everything.

It's the greatest privilege and joy of my life to see hearts transformed when faith and technology meet at the feet of Jesus. I'm so grateful to share this journey with you.

Introduction

Unlocking the Ancient Power of the Lord's Prayer

Welcome to the journey that could transform your life—unlocking the ancient, life-changing power of the Lord's Prayer.

Spoken by Jesus Himself (Matt. 6:9–13; Luke 11:2–4) these timeless words have echoed across centuries, continents, and cultures, uniting Christians of every tradition. More than just a familiar recitation, the Lord's Prayer is a profound invitation into deep intimacy with God—a blueprint for daily living shaped by trust, worship, forgiveness, and surrender.

When the disciples asked, "Lord, teach us to pray" (Luke 11:1), Jesus didn't just give them words to memorize; He offered them a way of life. From the earliest gatherings of believers to modern churches around the world—Orthodox, Catholic, Protestant, and beyond—this prayer has remained at the heart of Christian identity and practice.

Each phrase is rich with meaning:

> God as our loving Father
> His kingdom advancing through our lives
> Daily provision, offered freely
> Forgiveness that transforms our hearts
> Protection from temptation and deliverance from evil
> Glory given to God forever and ever

In just a few powerful lines, the Lord's Prayer captures the essence of Christian faith—and invites you to live it.

Throughout this book, we will walk step by step through the Lord's Prayer, not merely studying it but **inhabiting** it—building a vibrant house of prayer where God's presence can dwell deeply in your life. You will discover how these ancient words, spoken by Jesus Himself, still breathe life, hope, and power into every corner of our modern world.

Are you ready to unlock the treasure Jesus placed within your reach?

Let's begin—together.

Part 1

THE INVITATION

Building Your Spiritual Home

Chapter 1

Write the Vision

"Lord, teach us to pray."

Luke 11:1

Have you ever wondered why, out of all the incredible things Jesus did—walking on water, healing the blind, multiplying food—His disciples specifically asked Him to teach them to pray?

They didn't ask Him to show them how to preach or how to perform miracles. What they longed to understand was the source of His power ... and His peace. Prayer was Jesus' lifeline—the invisible bridge between heaven and earth. It anchored every miracle, every moment of compassion, every word He spoke.

What if you could discover that same lifeline?

What if prayer became your favorite place to live—not a duty, but a daily delight?

Finding Your Sacred Space

Everyone needs a special place to connect deeply with God. For you, it might be a quiet corner in your home, a park bench, or even your car parked beside a lake. For me, it's a forest trail near our house. As I walk beneath the trees, the words of Scripture come alive. And again and again, it's the words of the Lord's Prayer that guide me.

Step by step, I found myself praying, "Our Father ...," and something unexpected happened. Each phrase opened up a room in my heart—a place where God was waiting to meet me.

One day, while walking and praying, this idea came to me like a whisper:

> *Could the Lord's Prayer be more than a list of requests?*
> *Could it be a spiritual house?*

I began to see it—a structure, a dwelling, a sacred architecture made up of phrases. A house with two floors: the upper floor focused on God's glory, the lower floor focused on our daily needs. A staircase connecting the two. A roof. A foundation. And each line of the Lord's Prayer—another door, another room.

I shared this vision with Muriel, my wife, and then with close friends—pastors, artists, theologians. Their encouragement gave me the boldness to write what you're reading today.

A Life-Changing Encounter

Not long after that, I received an email from my friend Déborah Rosenkranz—the author of *Un Miracle Chaque Jour* in German. Her French mother had helped her translate a few devotional texts, and one landed right in my inbox.

It included this verse:

> Here is my greeting in my own handwriting—Paul. Remember my chains. (Col. 4:18 NLT)

That verse hit me hard. Paul wrote it from prison, likely with a hand chained, aching, wounded.

A hand once used to harm, now used to bring life.

A hand the world may have tried to silence, now used to speak hope.

Debbie added this reflection:

> That hand—the one once wounded, the one others tried to paralyze—became the very hand God used to write Scripture. What about your hand? Will you pick up the pen again? Will you let God write a story of healing through you?

That same day, I opened my laptop and started to write this book.

The Endless Adventure of Revelation

John ends his gospel with this breathtaking sentence:

> Jesus also did many other things. If they were all written down, I suppose the whole world could not contain the books that would be written. (John 21:25 NLT)

That verse still fills me with awe. God's truth is bottomless. His Word is eternal and living.

There are still books waiting to be written—and perhaps, you're meant to write one too.

One more verse ignited this fire within me:

> Write down the revelation
> and make it plain on tablets
> so that a herald may run with it. (Hab. 2:2)

So I wrote—not for myself only, but for anyone who wants to walk more deeply with God through prayer.

Rooted in Timeless Truth

Did you know Jesus' prayer life was deeply rooted in ancient Jewish traditions?

Every day, He prayed the Shema:

> Hear, O Israel: The LORD our God, the LORD is one. (Deut. 6:4)

Even the Lord's Prayer echoes the ancient Jewish prayers like the Kaddish, which speaks of God's name being honored, His kingdom coming, and His will being done.

Jesus wasn't erasing His heritage. He was fulfilling it—and offering us a simple, effective model to experience God's presence.

Emily shared, "Prayer is my safe space, an inner room where I'm completely loved and known. Here, God meets me exactly as I am."

Are You Ready for a Challenge?

Here's my invitation to you:

For the next thirty chapters, spend just ten intentional minutes each morning with God. Walk through your own sacred house of prayer—room by room—and see how He meets you.

What might happen if prayer became not something you do—but where you dwell?

Practical Steps Forward

- **Choose Your Sacred Space:** Find a quiet place to meet God each day.
- **Reflection Question:** Each morning ask, "Lord, what new revelation do You have for me today?"

Let's Pray Together

Heavenly Father,

Like the disciples, I say, "Lord, teach me to pray."

Transform the Lord's Prayer from familiar words into fresh fire.

Shape my life into a living house of prayer, where every thought, every breath becomes an offering.

Open my heart wide to hear Your voice.
Let my prayers rise like incense and return to earth with power.
I believe You are already waiting for me in each room.
Thank You for the invitation. I say yes.
In Jesus' mighty name, amen.

Where We Go from Here

As we begin this sacred journey, remember:

Prayer is not just a discipline—it's a divine invitation.

A door is open.

Step through it—heart first—and discover the treasure waiting inside.

Take a deeper dive into this chapter by listening to this podcast episode:

https://ericcelerier.net/podcast-1

Chapter 2

God's Doorway—a Personal Invitation

"In the beginning God created the heavens and the earth."

Genesis 1:1

Maybe you're like me—you tend to skip over introductions, thinking they're just formalities. But I'd like to encourage you to pause here. This chapter matters deeply to me, because it will help you understand the heart of this book and how it personally speaks into your life. Thank you for taking this moment together with me.

Did you know the very first letter of the first Hebrew word in the Bible is *beth*? In Hebrew, this letter shares its root with the word for "house," and even visually resembles an open home, warmly inviting us in.

Throughout this book, we'll explore a special kind of house—God's own house. This theme of a divine dwelling appears right from the first word of Scripture, and it's a home that God personally invites you into.

Certainly, this *beth* could symbolize earth, our shared home that shelters and nurtures us—a beautiful concept that Pope Francis explores in his encyclical *Laudato Si'*. However, here we'll primarily discover the spiritual significance of this house: your own spiritual home.

Welcomed by God Himself

Have you ever noticed the Bible itself starts with an invitation?

The very first word in Hebrew is *Bereshit*, translated as "In the beginning," begins precisely with this welcoming *beth*. Right from Scripture's first moment, God personally rolls out a divine welcome mat, inviting each one us into His presence.

This invitation carries profound meaning: God has always desired a dwelling place among His people. The image of a house is woven deeply through Scripture—from Eden, through Moses's tabernacle and Solomon's temple, right into the sanctuary of our hearts today.

> Martina shared, "The image of home at the start of the Lord's Prayer deeply touched me. It reminded me that I'm God's beloved child and gave me confidence to walk through life trusting in His limitless love."

Images That Illuminate Our Faith

Throughout my own times of meditation and prayer, I've noticed God often speaks through images, parables, and vivid metaphors. This way of communicating, especially common in Eastern cultures, helps simplify complex truths, making them easy to grasp and remember. When seen in this light, the Bible becomes a stunning collection of living images designed to inspire, guide, and bring us into harmony with God's heart.

Jesus, deeply rooted in Jewish tradition, frequently used these memorable images and parables to share wisdom. The Lord's Prayer itself, firmly grounded in that heritage, echoes and beautifully expands upon the ancient Jewish prayer known as the Kaddish. Through this, Jesus crafted a prayer that transcends.

The Hebrew word *Kaddish* means "sanctification," and it stands at the heart of Jewish worship, praising and magnifying the holiness of God's name.

Here's how the Kaddish begins and concludes:

> Magnified and sanctified be His great Name
> In the world He created according to His will.
> May He establish His kingdom,
> May His salvation flourish and may He bring near
> His anointed one ...
> Before their Father who is in heaven, and say Amen.

The parallels between these words—*Father*, *name*, *will*, *kingdom*, *heaven*, *amen*—and those we find in the Lord's Prayer are truly moving.

From Eden to Emmanuel

From Eden onward, God's deepest longing has always been clear: intimate communion with us. Eden was more than a garden—it was humanity's original spiritual home, a sacred place of unhindered fellowship with our Creator. Although sin disrupted this intimacy, God never ceased inviting us back home.

His invitation resounded through Moses's tabernacle and Solomon's temple and became perfectly clear through Jesus, Emmanuel—meaning "**God with us**."

God is the God who longs to dwell with His people, who desires intimacy above all.

Consider John 1:14:

> The Word became flesh and dwelt among us. (NKJV)

The Greek word translated as "dwelt" means to pitch a tent, bringing to mind the tabernacle in the wilderness. From the very beginning, God didn't just want to speak to us—He longed to dwell closely among us.

And now, through prayer, He makes His home within our hearts.

A House Built by Prayer

The Lord's Prayer, given to us directly by Jesus, is truly remarkable. Although concise—just about ten sentences and exactly sixty-six Greek words—it gracefully encapsulates the entire biblical story. It's fascinating how this brief prayer symbolically echoes the richness contained in the sixty-six books of the Protestant Bible.

Each phrase of the Lord's Prayer invites you into a special room within your heart, carefully crafted to lead you into deeper intimacy with the Father.

Tim Keller describes prayer wonderfully:

> Prayer turns theology into experience.[1]

Each word in the Lord's Prayer is crafted to transform ordinary moments into extraordinary encounters with God.

Evie testified, "For me, home wasn't always safe during childhood. But today, when I speak with my Father, I feel welcomed, loved, and valued beyond my deepest dreams. His love surrounds and heals me everywhere."

Your Personal Response

Why not pause right now and personally respond to God's invitation?

Take a quiet moment and honestly share with Him your feelings, hopes, or even struggles. Think of this as adding another intimate room to your spiritual house of prayer—a space where God truly loves to dwell.

Gently Guided by the Holy Spirit

Jesus promised the Holy Spirit will continuously lead us into deeper truths:

> The Advocate, the Holy Spirit, whom the Father will send in my name, will teach you all things and will remind you of everything I have said to you. (John 14:26)

Just as ancient rabbis studied Scripture as multifaceted gems, you too are invited into an ongoing journey of discovery, continually uncovering new treasures from God's Word.

Simple Steps to Grow

- **Instant Invitation:** Pause briefly now, and pray simply: "Father, dwell richly in my heart today."
- **Reflection Question:** Before bed tonight, gently ask yourself, "How did I experience God's invitation today?"

Let these simple practices deepen your awareness of God's loving presence and help foster a lasting intimacy with Him.

Let's Talk to God Together

Heavenly Father,

Thank You for personally inviting me closer, right from the very beginning. From Eden to today, intimacy with me has always been Your greatest desire. Please make my heart Your home, filled continually with Your presence.

Holy Spirit, guide me deeper into Your truth. Use the Lord's Prayer to transform my daily life into sacred encounters with You.

In Jesus' precious name, amen.

Where We Go from Here

This journey isn't just about learning prayers. It's about becoming a living house—a place God genuinely loves to dwell.

In the next chapter, we'll meet Jesus, our Master Architect—the one who deeply desires to design and fill every splendid room of your personal house of prayer.

Take a deeper dive into this chapter by listening to this podcast episode:

https://ericcelerier.net
/podcast-2

Chapter 3

The *Tekton*—Master Architect of Your Heart

Have you ever walked through a house being renovated? Dust covers everything, the noise can be deafening, and chaos often reigns. Yet beneath that apparent mess, something entrancing is quietly taking shape.

My spiritual journey has often felt exactly like this—messy, confusing, and at times even painful. But looking back, I clearly see now: every moment has been part of an intentional design, gently guided by Jesus—the Master Architect of my heart.

In previous chapters, we've explored God's deep desire for intimacy with us. Now let's meet Jesus, our *tekton*, who lovingly crafts our lives into His masterpiece.

More Than a Carpenter

For the first ten or fifteen years of His adult life, Jesus quietly worked as a carpenter in Nazareth. Yet the Greek word used to describe Him, *tekton*, means so much more than simply working with wood. A *tekton* was a skilled craftsman, a designer, someone who thoughtfully envisioned, planned, and constructed using a variety of materials.[1]

When people in Nazareth skeptically asked, "Isn't this the carpenter?" (Mark 6:3), their familiarity blinded them. They saw wood and nails, but Jesus saw transformed lives built for eternity.

When I first discovered the deeper meaning of *tekton*, it truly touched me. Jesus wasn't just fixing broken beams—He was carefully designing entire lives. Mine. Yours.

Greg Leith, CEO of Convene, once shared this insight:

> Jesus wasn't just a carpenter—He was a master planner. Today we would call Him an architect.[2]

A *tekton* doesn't simply work with tools; he works with vision.

> Emily authentically shared, "Seeing Jesus as my Master Architect changed how I approach life's storms. Every trial now feels purposeful, refining my character and deepening my faith."

Your Life Built on Rock

Jesus illustrates beautifully the importance of a solid foundation in His parable of the two builders (see Matt. 7:24–27). Both constructed houses, but only the house built on solid rock withstood the storms.

Take an honest moment and ask yourself, "What foundation is my life built on today?"

The Lord's Prayer isn't simply words to recite—it's a sturdy foundation that can anchor your heart deeply in God's truth.

Jesus invites us warmly:

> When you pray, go into your room, close the door and pray to your Father, who is unseen. (Matt. 6:6)

This "room" is your heart, intentionally designed for intimate communion with God. Stepping into this sacred space helps you shift:

- From performance to presence
- From distraction to divine intimacy

Authentic Intimacy over Performance

Jesus gently warns us:

> Do not be like the hypocrites.... They have received their reward in full. (Matt. 6:5)

Real prayer seeks intimacy with God, not applause from others. Your heart, personally crafted by the Master Architect, is meant to be a sanctuary—a sacred place to meet with Him privately.

Paul captures this truth delightfully:

> We are God's handiwork, created in Christ Jesus to do good works, which God prepared in advance for us to do. (Eph. 2:10)

The Greek word *poiēma*, translated as "handiwork," means "masterpiece."[3] You're not random or accidental; you're carefully and lovingly crafted by Jesus Himself.

When I realized how intentionally Jesus crafts our lives, another memorable image deeply resonated with me.

C. S. Lewis insightfully describes this truth:

> Imagine yourself as a living house. God comes in to rebuild that house.... You thought you were being made into a decent little cottage: but He is building a palace. He intends to come and live in it Himself.[4]

Like tectonic plates shifting beneath the surface (interestingly, the word *tectonic* comes from *tekton*), the Lord's Prayer has unseen power, gently transforming us from within. Even difficult moments, which I once viewed as setbacks, now feel purposeful—used lovingly by God to reshape my heart more into Christ's image.

Sophie added, "Realizing Jesus intentionally designs every detail of my life has brought incredible peace. Even in uncertainty, I completely trust His loving hands."

Your Personal Response

Take a quiet moment to honestly reflect:

- What area of your life urgently needs the Architect's loving touch today?
- Write it down clearly. Prayerfully place it before Him, trusting fully that Jesus will bring it to life within the blueprint of your heart.

When you practice these simple steps, you'll discover a deeper intimacy with God, lasting peace, and new strength to face life's storms with greater resilience.

Let's Talk to God Together

Heavenly Father,

Thank You for sending Jesus, the Master Architect of my heart. Today I open myself completely to Your loving design. Please gently remove anything in me that might block Your closeness. Transform my life into a vibrant, living house of prayer.

Jesus, reshape and renew every corner of my heart. Grant me clarity and courage to fully embrace Your amazing plan. Thank You for crafting me intentionally and with great love.

In Your precious name, amen.

Where We Go from Here

As we move into the next chapter, the Master Architect is ready to clear away distractions and deepen His renovation in your heart. Are you ready to welcome His transforming touch today?

Take a deeper dive into this chapter by listening to this podcast episode:

https://ericcelerier.net /podcast-3

Chapter 4

Overturning Tables

Have you ever stepped into a room so cluttered that your heart immediately sank?

I have—more than once. In fact, even as a pastor, I've found myself repeatedly in moments when my heart felt exactly like that chaotic room: crowded with anxieties, distractions, and misplaced priorities. My prayers had become routine and mechanical, and genuine intimacy with God seemed painfully distant.

Maybe you've experienced this too?

It was in those moments of honest realization that I knew exactly what I needed: I needed Jesus to passionately overturn the tables cluttering my spiritual life.

In previous chapters, we've seen Jesus gently shaping our hearts as the Master Architect. But sometimes, before He can build something truly inviting, He must first lovingly clear away the clutter.

A Passionate Cleansing

One of Scripture's most vivid scenes is Jesus entering the temple in Jerusalem:

> It is written, "My house will be called a house of prayer," but you are making it "a den of robbers." (Matt. 21:13)

When Jesus overturned those tables, He wasn't driven by uncontrolled anger. Instead, He acted with prophetic clarity and spiritual intentionality, restoring the temple's true purpose: intimate communion with God. Notice the symbolic power of His actions:

- **Overturned tables** meant the merchants had to get down on their knees to collect scattered coins—the humble, essential posture of prayer.
- **Freed doves** compelled everyone to lift their eyes toward heaven, reminding them of renewed spiritual connection.

This dynamic moment was remarkably portrayed by my friend Jonathan Roumie at the beginning of season 5 of *The Chosen*. Jonathan humorously confided to me that he was personally trained to handle the whip by the same expert who taught Harrison Ford for *Indiana Jones*. He even kept the whip afterward ... "just in case"!

Your Heart: God's Sacred Dwelling

Long before Jesus cleansed the physical temple, God declared through the prophet Isaiah:

> These I will bring to my holy mountain
> and give them joy in my house of prayer …
> a house of prayer for all nations. (56:7)

Look carefully at these words:

- **My house:** Your heart is God's chosen home.
- **House of prayer:** Its purpose is ongoing, sacred conversation.
- **For all nations:** No one is excluded.
- **Joy:** Genuine prayer brings delight, not duty.

Today, Jesus desires to reclaim your heart with the same clarity and intentionality. Paul reminds us:

> Do you not know that your bodies are temples of the Holy Spirit, who is in you …? (1 Cor. 6:19)

But let's be honest—our hearts easily become cluttered. That's precisely where Jesus steps in—not with harsh condemnation but with gentle, cleansing love.

Mark confessed that chasing status had left him empty. When he finally surrendered his clutter to Jesus, quiet joy returned—real and lasting.

What about You?

Maybe you've been building a life that looks impressive—but what about your soul?

Years ago, I met a man who seemed to have everything: a vast wine collection, a private elevator, every imaginable luxury. Yet, spiritually, he was empty. Sadly, he passed away shortly after, never truly enjoying what he had accumulated.

Jesus told a parable that reminds us of this truth:

> [A rich man said] "I'll say to myself, 'You have plenty of grain laid up for many years. Take life easy; eat, drink and be merry.'"
>
> But God said to him, "You fool! This very night your life will be demanded from you. Then who will get what you have prepared for yourself?" (Luke 12:19–20)

And Jesus concluded with a sobering reflection:

> This is how it will be with whoever stores up things for themselves but is not rich toward God. (v. 21)

Reflect personally:

- Where are your true treasures today?
- What genuinely fills your heart?
- Are you rich toward God?

Interactive Moment: Heart Inventory

Take a quiet moment now.

- What tables in your life need to be overturned?
- What distractions, worries, or ambitions crowd out intimacy with God?

Write them down clearly, and then pray: "Jesus, with Your loving authority, overturn every distraction. Reclaim my heart fully for Yourself."

Simple Steps Forward

- **Daily Prayer:** "Jesus, clear the distractions from my heart today."
- **Evening Reflection:** Regularly ask yourself: "Did I live today as a true house of prayer?"
- **Weekly Clean-Out:** Take a few minutes to journal about any clutter you notice, intentionally surrendering it to Jesus.

A Powerful Perspective

John Ortberg wisely reminds us:

> God isn't interested in your "spiritual life." God is just interested in your life. He intends to redeem it.[1]

God desires to dwell in every room of your heart—not just those labeled "religious."

Let's Pray Together

Heavenly Father,

Just as Jesus lovingly reclaimed the temple, please reclaim my heart today. Overturn every table of distraction, fear, or selfish ambition. Let my heart become Your true house of prayer—a place You love to dwell.

Thank You for Your passionate, persistent love. Teach me each day to welcome You freely, to release my clutter willingly, and to trust Your restoring hands completely.

In Jesus' powerful name, amen.

Laura shared how chronic illness had worn her down spiritually. Slowly praying the Lord's Prayer reopened the sacred space in her heart.

Where We Go from Here

As Jesus lovingly clears your heart's clutter, He makes room for something truly wonderful.

In the next chapter, we'll embrace childlike simplicity and wonder, discovering the fresh blueprint God has for your heart.

Are you ready to see what He builds next?

Take a deeper dive into this chapter by listening to this podcast episode:

https://ericcelerier.net/podcast-4

Chapter 5

Blueprint of the Heart

Do you remember the pure joy you felt as a child, holding a box of crayons, facing a blank page with endless possibilities?

Jesus once prayed:

> I praise you, Father, Lord of heaven and earth, because you have hidden these things from the wise and learned, and revealed them to little children. (Matt. 11:25)

Childlike faith isn't immaturity—it's spiritual clarity. It's openness, trust, and wonder. Often, rediscovering God's vision for our lives doesn't begin with deep theology but with something as simple and appealing as a child's drawing.

Proudly Showing Your Drawing

Imagine being a child again, proudly showing your drawing to your dad: "Look, Daddy! I drew our house. Here's the door, here's the window, and here's the chimney. And here's Mommy, and you, Daddy. Oh, and look—I added the sun and a tree! Isn't it wonderful?"

Do you remember your own first drawings? Maybe, like me, you began by sketching stick figures before bravely drawing your very first house.

This reminds me of a famous scene from Antoine de Saint-Exupéry's *The Little Prince*. The little prince asks the aviator, "Draw me a sheep." After several unsatisfactory attempts, the aviator finally draws a simple box and explains, "The sheep is inside." The little prince's face lights up with delight.

This wonderful interaction highlights how children effortlessly use their imagination. It shows us the beauty and power of simplicity—a quality we should all treasure in our hearts.

Deanna envisioned, "In my drawing, there's a garden full of flowers representing prayers and worship. It's where we gather as a family, loved and growing together."

My First Communion: A Sacred Encounter

I clearly remember preparing for my first communion at ten years old. Honestly, I didn't fully grasp its spiritual meaning—I mostly wanted the yellow bicycle my parents promised me. But something unexpected happened.

On that day, I encountered the living presence of Jesus. The forgiveness and peace I experienced were so moving that the bicycle faded into the background. It became one of the most sacred and cherished memories of my life—a strong demonstration of childlike faith in action.

The Power of Simplicity

We have much to learn by studying children. They know how to live each day with joy, to trust fully, and to embrace the mystery of God without needing all the answers.

Jesus emphasized this clearly:

> Truly I tell you, unless you change and become like little children, you will never enter the kingdom of heaven. (Matt. 18:3)

Childlike faith gently opens the door to God's kingdom, allowing us to embrace spiritual truths often hidden by complexity.

Sketch Your House of Prayer

Here's a creative challenge: Take a pen and paper, and sketch your house of prayer. Don't worry about artistic skill—this is about spiritual vision. Perhaps your house has open windows to welcome the Holy Spirit or a garden full of flowers symbolizing praise. Or maybe it's just a simple box—but you know God is there, ready to meet you.

The Hebrew word for "house," *bayith*, means more than a building. It speaks of family, legacy, and sacred dwelling.

When King David wanted to build God a house, God turned the promise around and gave David a lasting spiritual legacy (see 2 Sam. 7:11–13).

Your sketch isn't just child's play—it's a heartfelt prayer saying, "Lord, here's my heart. Dwell here."

If you'd like, I'd love to see your drawing. Feel free to email it to me at contact@ericcelerier.net. It always brings me joy to see how others visualize their heart as a house of prayer.

> John expressed, "My prayer house is strong and stable—a temple that withstands storms. It anchors me in God, always firm and unshakable."

Filled with God's Fullness

Paul offers this heartfelt prayer for us:

> [I pray] that Christ may **dwell** in your hearts through faith ... that you ... may ... grasp how wide and long and high and deep is the love of Christ, and to know this love that surpasses knowledge—that you may be **filled** to the measure of all the **fullness of God**. (Eph. 3:17–19)

- **Dwell** (*katoikeō*)**:** Christ wants to comfortably live in you.
- **Filled** (*plēroō*)**:** Completely saturated by God's presence.
- **Fullness of God:** Nothing missing—overflowing life.

Your drawing becomes a visible reminder of this invisible truth.

Simple Ways to Grow in Childlike Faith

Here are some heartfelt ways to practice childlike simplicity this week:

- **Sketch Your Prayer House:** Place it somewhere visible, reminding you daily that your heart welcomes God's presence.
- **Reflect:** Which aspect of childlike faith do you wish you could rediscover today? Write it down and talk honestly with God about it.

As you embrace these simple practices, you'll find your heart becoming lighter, clearer, and more open to the joy of being deeply known by God.

Let's Talk to God Together

Heavenly Father,

Like a child offering a drawing, I offer You my heart today. Restore the joy and wonder of childlike faith within me. Show me again the beauty of simplicity.

Jesus, live comfortably and freely within me. Expand my heart until it's overflowing with Your love.

Holy Spirit, help me draw not just with my hands but with my whole life. May each day become a fresh blueprint filled with Your grace, joy, and presence.

In Jesus' name, amen.

Where We Go from Here

As we journey forward, watch how God transforms these simple, heartfelt sketches into vibrant, Spirit-filled dwellings.

He's not just accepting your drawing—He's eagerly preparing to inhabit it. Are you ready to build with Him today?

Take a deeper dive into this chapter by listening to this podcast episode:

https://ericcelerier.net/podcast-5

Chapter 6

You Are His Dwelling

Have you ever experienced a moment when God's presence became strikingly real, reshaping your entire understanding of Him?

Imagine being alone, feeling overwhelmed by life's pressures, when suddenly, a comforting truth whispers into your heart: "You are the temple of the living God." In an instant, your burdens lift, peace floods your heart, and the ordinary space around you transforms into a sacred sanctuary.

This realization—that God Himself chooses to dwell within you permanently—can radically change not just a moment but your entire life.

In our previous chapter, we envisioned our hearts as houses of prayer with childlike simplicity. Yet God desires more than sketches—He longs for your life itself to become His vibrant, living dwelling, filled with His presence and glory.

God's Passionate Pursuit

Since the garden of Eden, God's deepest desire has always been clear: He wants to dwell among His people. Eden was not just paradise; it was a sacred place where God walked and spoke personally with humanity (see Gen. 3:8). Though sin disrupted that intimacy, God never stopped pursuing restoration. From the moment He asked, "Where are you?" He's been inviting us back into communion.

Throughout history, He provided compelling signs of His longing:

- The tabernacle, a portable house of prayer, called the "tent of meeting" (Ex. 33:7).
- A divine blueprint given to Moses: "Make this tabernacle and all its furnishings exactly like the pattern I will show you" (Ex. 25:9).

Even King Solomon, in building the great temple, humbly recognized its limits:

> Will God really dwell on earth? The heavens, even the highest heaven, cannot contain you. How much less this temple I have built! (1 Kings 8:27)

Paul echoes this with clarity:

> The God who made the world and everything in it ... does not live in temples built by human hands. (Acts 17:24)

God isn't looking for stone structures. Instead, He's lovingly constructing a spiritual house—brick by brick, heart by heart.

Your Heart—God's True Dwelling

Paul reminds us clearly:

> Don't you know that you yourselves are God's temple and that God's Spirit dwells in your midst? (1 Cor. 3:16)

Peter affirms warmly:

> You also, like living stones, are being built into a spiritual house. (1 Pet. 2:5)

And Hebrews emphasizes gently:

> We are his house, if indeed we hold firmly to our confidence and the hope in which we glory. (3:6)

You yourself—body, mind, and spirit—are God's chosen dwelling. His Spirit isn't just a guest; He desires to make His permanent home within you.

From Dwelling to Glory

Ezekiel's vision gives us a powerful glimpse of what God desires for us:

> The glory of the LORD rose ... [and] filled the temple,... full of the radiance of the glory of the LORD. (10:4)

This Old Testament image foreshadows the reality God wants for your heart today—not mere occupancy but complete fullness. Not just a gentle whisper but an overwhelming presence.

You are the place where God chose to dwell. You are His home. You are His sanctuary. It's in the deepest center of your being that He delights to abide.

Abide—Not Just Visit

Jesus personally invites us:

> If you remain in me and my words remain in you, ask whatever you wish, and it will be done for you. (John 15:7)

The word *remain* ("abide") means to make your home, to make your permanent home. God is calling you into a continuous relationship of intimacy, not just occasional visits.

> Olivia wrote genuinely, "Knowing that God chose my heart as His home infused my days with genuine purpose. His presence now guides every decision I make."

Practical Steps for Welcoming His Presence

- **Declare Daily:** "Father, remind me today that I am Your dwelling. Fill every part of my life with Your presence."

- **Pause and Reflect Regularly:** "Am I honoring God's presence within me right now?"
- **Weekly Meditation:** Read Ephesians 3:17–19, visualizing your heart being filled completely with His presence and love.

As you internalize these simple practices, you'll notice a deeper peace settling into your heart. You'll become naturally aware of God's presence throughout each day, discover renewed purpose in your relationships, and find yourself longing to grow closer and deeper in your walk with Him.

Valerie reflected warmly, "It's an unspeakable joy to realize that the Holy Spirit actually lives in me. My prayer is simply to become a place He truly delights to dwell in."

Let's Pray Together

Heavenly Father,

Thank You for choosing my heart as Your home. It amazes me that You—the God who fills heaven and earth—desire to dwell intimately within me.

Fill me anew today with Your Spirit. Let Your presence saturate every part of my life, shaping my heart into a place where You love to live.

Jesus, let Your words remain deeply within me. Turn my ordinary daily moments into simple, genuine acts of worship.

Holy Spirit, don't let me settle for occasional visits. Dwell in me fully. Let every thought, word, and action reflect Your love and grace.

In Jesus' powerful and loving name, amen.

Where We Go from Here

You are not merely a follower of Christ—you are His dwelling place. And God's blueprint for your life is filled with intimacy, wonder, and divine presence.

In the next chapter, we'll begin uncovering the deeper mystery hidden within the Lord's Prayer—discovering how each phrase opens a door to divine presence and revelation.

Take a deeper dive into this chapter by listening to this podcast episode:

https://ericcelerier.net/podcast-6

Are you ready to open your heart and fully welcome Him home?

Chapter 7

Unlocking the Divine Mystery

Have you ever encountered something familiar that suddenly revealed itself as altogether new, shifting your entire understanding?

Maybe it was a Scripture verse you've read countless times, a simple prayer you've repeated for years, or a childhood story—yet in one unexpected moment, it came alive, transforming your heart. The Lord's Prayer is exactly this kind of divine mystery, continually inviting us into deeper intimacy with God.

A mystery is like a pearl—it reveals its beauty only to those who know its value. Even Einstein once said:

> The most beautiful experience we can have is the mysterious.[1]

While he explored the physical universe, we are invited to explore the mysteries of God. Pastor Timothy Keller puts it this way:

> Prayer turns theology into experience.[2]

The Lord's Prayer isn't meant to be merely recited—it's a doorway. A blueprint. An invitation to experience God's presence in ever-deepening ways.

Stepping into the Mystery

What makes the Lord's Prayer so extraordinary is its endless depth, always revealing more to those who seek. Let's step now into this sacred mystery.

Jesus often taught through parables—simple stories holding hidden depth. Why? Because God treasures discovery. The Greek word for "mystery," *mustērion*, means a secret that is hidden for a time but destined to be revealed.[3]

Jesus told His disciples:

> The knowledge of the secrets of the kingdom of heaven has been given to you. (Matt. 13:11)

Paul echoed:

> The mystery [was] made known to me by revelation.... You will be able to understand my insight into the mystery of Christ. (Eph. 3:3–4)

And again:

> This, then, is how you ought to regard us: as servants of Christ and as those entrusted with the mysteries God has revealed. (1 Cor. 4:1)

Each phrase in the Lord's Prayer is like a room in a great house—waiting to be entered, explored, and inhabited.

Hearts Ablaze on the Road to Emmaus

Remember the disciples walking toward Emmaus? Discouraged, disoriented, unaware that Jesus was beside them. He opened the Scriptures, showing them how everything pointed to Him. Then came the moment:

> When he was at the table with them, he took bread, gave thanks, broke it and began to give it to them. Then their eyes were opened and they recognized him. (Luke 24:30–31)

And their response?

> Were not our hearts burning within us while he talked with us on the road and opened the Scriptures to us? (v. 32)

This is what God desires for you: that every time you pray the Lord's Prayer, your heart would burn, your eyes would open, and you would recognize Him.

Antoinette put it this way: "Sometimes I have to read a passage several times before I truly grasp it. It's like walking into a house—first you're on the porch, then in the hallway, then the kitchen. Every prayer reveals a new room."

From Blindness to Sight

Like the man healed in John 9, who said, "I was blind but now I see" (v. 25), revelation changes everything. What once felt routine becomes radiant. What felt hidden becomes holy.

Practical Steps Forward

- **Daily Revelation Invitation:** Before praying, whisper, "Lord, reveal something new to me today."
- **Phrase Meditation:** Choose one phrase from the Lord's Prayer. Ask God, "What hidden truth do You want me to see here?"
- **Reflection Question:** What hidden truth about God or prayer do you most deeply desire to discover right now?

Let's Pray Together

Heavenly Father,

Thank You for hiding treasures in plain sight. Open my eyes as I pray. Let my heart burn within me as You reveal Jesus through every word. Draw me deeper into the mystery of Your love.

Holy Spirit, help me enter each room of this divine house with wonder. Show me what I've never seen before. Let every prayer become a place of encounter.

Jesus, break the bread of Your Word in my heart. Let me recognize You there.

In Your powerful name, amen.

> Nathan said, "Experiencing the mystery of the Lord's Prayer revolutionized my spiritual life. Prayer shifted from duty to daily delight."

Where We Go from Here

As we step forward, let's unlock the treasures hidden within each phrase Jesus taught us. In the next chapter, we begin with the most intimate words: "Our Father."

Are you ready to walk through the door?

Take a deeper dive into this chapter by listening to this podcast episode:

https://ericcelerier.net/podcast-7

A Sacred Pause before We Continue

Before stepping into the next part of our journey, let's pause for something truly special.

As a global ambassador for *The Chosen*, it is my privilege to share with you **Jonathan Roumie**—the actor portraying Jesus—reciting the Our Father prayer in Aramaic, the very language Jesus would have spoken.

This was recorded during the filming of the impactful scene depicting the feeding of the five thousand.

As you listen, you will feel yourself transported into a different world—a more ancient world—where prayer wasn't polished or formal but alive, intimate, and deeply connected to the Father.

Of course, no one knows the exact pronunciation of Aramaic from two thousand years ago. But the heart of this moment isn't about perfect words—it's about entering into the spirit of prayer that Jesus taught.

Let your heart imagine Jesus gently teaching you: "When you pray, say ..."

Feel the simplicity. The nearness. The invitation.

This moment is a bridge—between what we've discovered so far and what we are about to enter: **the sacred place where prayer truly begins ... in the arms of our heavenly Father.**

Let's walk forward together.

https://ericcelerier.net
/jonathanroumie

Reflection and Prayer

Reflection and Prayer

Part 2

WHERE PRAYER BEGINS

Meeting the Father

Chapter 8

Stepping into the Spiritual House

Recently, my wife and I visited Notre Dame of Paris following its long-awaited reopening. Years before, fire had devastated this iconic building. Yet, standing inside once again, I was deeply moved by what I saw: the cathedral, now restored, radiated a beauty far surpassing even its former glory. Sunlight streamed through restored windows, illuminating ancient stones polished by centuries of prayer. Awe and wonder flooded our hearts.

In a similar way, imagine something even greater—your life—as a spiritual sanctuary, lovingly designed and rebuilt by God Himself. Psalm 127:1 reminds us:

> Unless the LORD builds the house,
> the builders labor in vain.

Your life, anchored in Christ, is precisely this sacred dwelling—a masterpiece being continually shaped by divine hands. Just as Notre

Dame's beauty was restored beyond its original splendor, God desires to rebuild your heart into something even more radiant.

Approaching the Divine Door

Picture the entrance to your spiritual house. The door isn't at ground level but mysteriously suspended between heaven and earth. Invisible to the outside world, it becomes clear only through the eyes of faith, revealed by the Holy Spirit. This door is Jesus Himself.

> I am the gate; whoever enters through me will be saved. They will come in and go out, and find pasture. (John 10:9)

Jesus is the living doorway between divine purpose and our earthly lives. Through Him, you enter a place where routine becomes revelation and ordinary moments become filled with heavenly meaning.

Ascending to the Upper Level: A Cathedral Roof Open to Heaven

As you enter your spiritual house, your eyes naturally lift upward. Imagine a ceiling rising like the vast roof of a cathedral, open to heaven, drawing your spirit closer to God. This is precisely where the Lord's Prayer begins:

> Our Father in heaven ...

On this upper floor, everything reflects God's holiness, His kingdom, and His perfect will. This is a place of worship, reverence, and surrender.

> There will be no more night ... for the Lord God will give them light. And they will reign forever and ever. (Rev. 22:5)

Annika shared her experience: "These vast skies above me bring me to tears. They remind me of His holiness, His beauty, and His coming kingdom."

The Central Corridor: Heaven Touching Earth

Connecting the upper and lower levels of your house of prayer is a central staircase. Imagine it as a sacred passage called "on earth as it is in heaven." From here, a magnificent double staircase extends upward and downward, symbolizing the flow of love and grace between heaven and our daily lives.

Each room upstairs—God's name, kingdom, and will—is mirrored in the rooms downstairs: our daily needs, forgiveness, and deliverance. This divine symmetry reminds us that everything good originates from heaven and is intended to flow into our everyday experiences.

> Every good and perfect gift is from above, coming down from the Father of the heavenly lights. (James 1:17)

Ground Floor: Grace in Everyday Life

On the ground level, heaven's grace meets daily realities: your job, your family, your emotions. It's here that forgiveness is practiced, trust is built, and faith touches every aspect of life.

Underneath lies your foundation—often unseen but crucially important—built upon Scripture, trust, and daily dependence on God.

> We are God's handiwork, created in Christ Jesus to do good works, which God prepared in advance for us to do. (Eph. 2:10)

Sanctuary of Grace: A Personal Story

After thirty intense years of ministry, my wife and I took a much-needed sabbatical. An old friend, Adam, graciously offered us his house in Colorado. It was stunning: two floors, a spacious staircase, panoramic mountain views. We didn't realize at first that this gorgeous place would soon become a sanctuary for fresh dreams and ideas. It was there that God stirred my heart, calling me to launch *A Miracle Every Day*, and to fervently pray for a man named Jean-Pierre and his wife Chantal—prayers that later gave birth to the media movement called ZeWatchers, instrumental in bringing *The Chosen* series to France and beyond.

> Charlotte told me, "Visualizing this spiritual house inside me changed everything. Prayer isn't something complicated—it's simply stepping through that divine door and ascending the staircase toward heaven."

That Colorado home was an incredible gift. Yet even more precious is the house God continues building within me—a sanctuary from which new blessings flow: ideas, prayers, breakthroughs. I wonder, What dreams, prayers, and blessings might emerge from your own spiritual house of prayer?

Practical Steps Forward

- **Daily Step:** Begin your prayers today by consciously stepping through the door of Jesus, praying, "Jesus, today I enter fully into my spiritual house through You."
- **Visualization Practice:** Clearly picture your inner staircase. As your prayers rise with trust and love, visualize God's grace and answers gently descending into every part of your life.
- **Reflection:** Take a moment to reflect honestly: Is there an area of your life you're still hesitant to fully entrust to God's transforming presence?

Let's Pray Together

Heavenly Father,

Thank You for lovingly building this sacred home within me.

Jesus, You are the doorway into deeper intimacy and purpose—lead me into Your presence today.

Lift my eyes upward, Lord, toward the open roof filled with Your glory and beauty. May love and grace flow freely between heaven and every area of my life.

Holy Spirit, strengthen my foundations, bless each room, and gently reveal anything hidden. Transform my heart into a vibrant house of prayer—one You delight to dwell in.

In Jesus' name, amen.

Where We Go from Here

In the next chapter, we step through the first delightful room under the open cathedral ceiling: "Our Father."

It's the place where your divine identity becomes clear. Are you ready to draw closer to the Father's heart?

Take a deeper dive into this chapter by listening to this podcast episode:

https://ericcelerier.net/podcast-8

Chapter 9

The Father's Doorway

"Our Father in heaven."

Matthew 6:9

After stepping into your spiritual house, pause for a moment and lift your eyes toward the highest point—the soaring cathedral ceiling that opens directly toward heaven. Beneath this divine canopy, Jesus gently teaches us to begin our prayer not by focusing on ourselves but by turning our attention upward—toward the one who loves us perfectly: **our Father**.

The very first word Jesus places on our lips is not a request but a relationship: *Father*.

The Prayer Begins with the Father

In the original Greek, the Lord's Prayer begins directly with the word *Pater*—"Father." This intentional focus is crucial: prayer starts not with our needs, worries, or even worship but with recognizing who He truly is. Jesus places "Father" as the doorway into the entire prayer, reminding us that everything flows from intimacy with Him.

A Revolutionary Relationship

In Jesus' culture, no rabbi had dared address God with such intimacy. The Aramaic term Jesus used, *Abba*, wasn't formal—it was deeply personal, a child's trusting call to their parent. Before Jesus, Scripture never recorded anyone addressing God directly as Abba.

Jesus broke the mold. Throughout the Gospels, Jesus refers to the Father over two hundred times, constantly emphasizing their intimacy.

> The Son can do nothing by himself; he can do only what he sees his Father doing. (John 5:19)

> I and the Father are one. (John 10:30)

> Believe me when I say that I am in the Father and the Father is in me. (John 14:11)

Even in the deep agony of Gethsemane, Jesus prayed:

> *Abba*, Father ... everything is possible for You. Take this cup from me. Yet not what I will, but what you will. (Mark 14:36)

Remarkably, the only moment when Jesus didn't call God "Father" was on the cross:

> My God, my God, why have you forsaken me? (Matt. 27:46)

At that precise moment, Jesus bore our sins and our separation so that we could forever experience closeness and reconciliation with our Father.

Adopted into His Family

Paul invitingly explains our new identity:

> Because you are his sons, God sent the Spirit of his Son into our hearts, the Spirit who calls out, "*Abba*, Father." (Gal. 4:6)

> The Spirit you received does not make you slaves, so that you live in fear again; rather, the Spirit you received brought about your adoption to sonship. And by him we cry, "*Abba*, Father." (Rom. 8:15)

Through Christ, we aren't merely forgiven—we're adopted. That means full access, full inheritance, and full belonging. Your Father isn't distant or indifferent; He delights in you deeply.

Healing the Father Wound

For many, the word *father* can be complicated, even painful. Perhaps your earthly father was absent, harsh, or distant, casting shadows over your view of God.

Luke openly shared his experience:

> When I was young, my dad left. I respected him, but he wasn't present. For years I projected that

> absence onto God. It took a full spiritual renewal to realize my heavenly Father never leaves, always knows me, and longs for closeness. Now I remind myself daily: God is my true Father—with a capital *F*.

Mariah offered another perspective:

> Until age eighteen, I never called anyone "Daddy." I saw God as a distant judge, not a father. But during a prayer gathering, I finally cried out—and His love flooded my heart like never before. Slowly but surely, I began calling Him 'Daddy' with peace.

Contrast this with Mark's testimony, whose loving earthly father became a model of God's kindness:

> I was fortunate; my father was patient, gentle, and present. His example made it easier to trust God's love, but I also realized even my dad's best moments were just shadows of my heavenly Father's perfect love.

Whatever your experience, God's arms remain wide open. His love is constant, patiently waiting to heal and restore.

Discovering the Secret Place

Psalm 91:1 in the Darby translation says:

> He that dwelleth in the secret place of the Most High shall abide under the shadow of the Almighty.

That secret dwelling is your house of prayer, your meeting place with your Father. It's where His love replaces your fears and where closeness erases shame.

Practical Steps Forward

- **Reflect Honestly:** What barriers or past wounds might still prevent you from fully receiving God's fatherly love? Write them down, then offer them openly in prayer.
- **Personal Declaration:** Each day, declare aloud: "Father, I choose today to trust Your perfect love for me."
- **Visualization Practice:** Imagine yourself stepping closer to your heavenly Father. Picture His warm embrace, His welcoming eyes, and His voice affirming, "You are My beloved child."

Let's Pray Together

Abba Father,

Thank You for welcoming me into Your family. Thank You for adopting me, choosing me, and calling me Your beloved child.

Heal any wounds that still make it hard for me to trust Your love fully. Replace the hurt from absence or pain with the strength of Your constant, perfect affection. Let Your voice of love become louder and clearer than any fear or insecurity I carry.

Let me dwell in Your secret place, under the shadow of Your wings. Let the word *Father* awaken joy, security, and awe.

Let me find shelter in Your secret place, under the shadow of Your wings. Let calling You "Father" fill my heart with joy, security, and awe. Today, I embrace my identity as Your child, I receive Your perfect embrace, and from my heart I call You "Abba."

In Jesus' precious name, amen.

Where We Go from Here

You've just crossed the threshold of the Father's heart. You've learned to approach Him not with fear or formality but with trust—like a child running into the arms of their Father.

Take a deeper dive into this chapter by listening to this podcast episode:

https://ericcelerier.net/podcast-9

Now the journey takes you deeper. Before any request, before any worship, Jesus teaches us to begin our prayers with two simple words: *Our Father.*

What if those words weren't just an opening but an invitation—into family, into unity, into a love that holds us all together?

In the next chapter, we take our place at the family table.

Chapter 10

Invited to the Family Table

"Our Father in heaven."

Matthew 6:9

This is the first room on the upper floor of your house of prayer, a space beneath the cathedral roof of divine worship.

Remembering the Family Table

I clearly recall special dinners from my childhood—the inviting aroma of freshly baked baguettes, laughter echoing around our family table, and an overwhelming sense of belonging. These precious memories remind me how deeply we are designed for community. Those family dinners were more than just meals; they shaped my understanding of belonging, unity, and shared identity—exactly what Jesus conveys when teaching us to pray, "Our Father."

When Jesus taught these words, He wasn't simply giving us a formula; He was inviting us into an eternal gathering around God's table of grace.

The Power of "Our"

Why did Jesus teach us to say "our Father" and not "my Father"? Because, from the very first word, He was including us. He wasn't merely introducing His own relationship—He was welcoming us into it. "Our" means shared identity, shared inheritance, shared love.

This simple word gently yet completely levels the ground. It reminds us that God is not the exclusive possession of any denomination, tradition, or nation. He is the Father of all who draw near to Him in humility.

Breaking Down Walls

In Luke 18:9–14, Jesus tells a striking story about a Pharisee and a tax collector who went to the temple to pray. The Pharisee proudly thanked God that he was better than others. But the tax collector, filled with remorse, quietly prayed, "God, have mercy on me, a sinner." It was this humble man—not the proud Pharisee—who returned home justified.

Praying "our Father" keeps us grounded. We don't own God. We don't earn our place. We're not better than anyone else. We are fellow sinners, saved by the same grace.

A Sacred Encounter at Mount Athos

A few years ago, I visited Mount Athos, a deeply traditional Orthodox Christian sanctuary. Coming from an evangelical background, I initially found the icons, incense, and repetition of "Kyrie Eleison" foreign. But during a candlelight vigil, I felt God whisper gently into my heart, "These are My children too. They call Me Father, just as you do."

That night, I sensed the same warmth, acceptance, and belonging I'd experienced around my childhood family table. Through centuries of history, believers from every tradition—Orthodox, Catholic, Protestant—have lifted the same words toward heaven: "Our Father." In that sacred moment, I felt the unbreakable bond transcending traditions and generations.

> Patricia, a Catholic mother whose daughter attends an evangelical church, gave this insight: "What matters most to me is our relationship with God—not our religious label. 'Our Father' is a prayer of unity, reminding us to respect and love one another."

A Family without Borders

I once stood by the Sea of Galilee, guiding the president of a nation and his family through a spiritual journey. On the very mount where Jesus first taught the Lord's Prayer, we recited its words together. At that instant, I sensed God smiling over His family—a family without borders, united not by language, politics, or theology but by the Spirit.

Paul David Tripp captures this concept:

> The church is not a theological classroom. It is a conversion, confession, repentance, reconciliation, forgiveness, and sanctification center, where flawed people place their faith in Christ, gather to know and love Him better, and learn to love others as He designed.[1]

Praying With Humility and Wonder

God hears your prayers, but He also hears the prayers of others who worship differently. People speaking different languages or coming from a varied tradition—He loves them just as deeply. No one has exclusive access; all are equally invited.

Only the Holy Spirit teaches us to truly say "Abba"—not just for ourselves but for every soul the Father calls His own.

Seen, Known, and Loved

Though you are part of a vast, diverse family, your heavenly Father knows you intimately. He recognizes your voice. He treasures each tear you shed (see Ps. 56:8). He loves you as if you were the only person on earth—and He loves the entire world just as fully. That is the beautiful mystery of our Father.

Jacob gave this insight: "Participating in international prayer gatherings revealed the beauty and diversity of God's family, humbling me and filling me with gratitude."

Practical Steps to Foster Unity

- **Pray beyond Yourself:** Regularly pray for believers from other cultures, denominations, and traditions.
- **Visualize the Family Table:** When you pray, picture yourself at God's table, surrounded by a wonderfully diverse faith community.
- **Reflection Question:** What practical step can you take this week to strengthen your connection with God's broader family?
- **Introspective Challenge:** Is there anyone you've unconsciously excluded from the family of God—in your prayers, thoughts, or attitudes?

Each small step you take toward unity brings you closer to the heart of your Father, who delights deeply in the rich diversity of His family.

Let's Pray Together

Heavenly Father,

Thank You for inviting me to Your family table. Thank You for being not just my Father but *our* Father. Thank You for hearing every voice, holding every heart, and welcoming each of us with the same love.

Please tear down any walls of pride, prejudice, and self-righteousness I've built. Teach me to celebrate different expressions of faith, to seek true unity, and to honor Your image in every believer.

May each time I say "Our Father" become a declaration of belonging—not only to You but to Your beautiful family around the world. Build this room in my spiritual house into a place of unity, humility, and love.

In Jesus' precious name, amen.

Where We Go from Here

Now, with our hearts united around God's family table, let's lift our eyes even higher. In the next chapter, we'll explore what it means that our Father reigns in heaven.

Are you ready to deepen your awe and intimacy with Him?

Take a deeper dive into this chapter by listening to this podcast episode:

https://ericcelerier.net/podcast-10

Chapter 11

Our Father in Heaven

"Our Father in heaven,
hallowed be your name."
Matthew 6:9

Have you ever paused to truly consider what it means that your Father resides in heaven?

We've celebrated the warmth of calling God "Abba" and rejoiced in being part of His global family. Now Jesus invites us to lift our gaze higher—to the breathtaking reality of heaven itself.

Your prayers aren't merely private conversations; they're dynamic encounters with the Creator who lovingly rules from heaven's throne.

A Heavenly Perspective

When Jesus taught us to pray "Our Father in heaven," He wasn't describing a distant, disconnected deity. He unveiled a profound truth: our loving Father is also the sovereign ruler of the cosmos.

The Greek word Jesus uses for "heaven"—*ouranoîs*—is plural, encompassing:

- The blue sky above
- The starry heavens of galaxies and space
- The third heaven—the unseen realm where God's throne and eternal kingdom reside

> To the LORD your God belong the heavens, even the highest heavens, the earth and everything in it. (Deut. 10:14)

> Will God really dwell on earth? The heavens, even the highest heaven, cannot contain you. (1 Kings 8:27)

Think about this: the very same God who spoke galaxies into existence intentionally formed and deeply cherishes you.

Paul encourages us to lift our hearts:

> Set your hearts on things above, where Christ is, seated at the right hand of God. (Col. 3:1)

This almighty God is not remote—He is thoroughly aware of your struggles, deeply attentive to your prayers, and tenderly involved in every detail of your daily life.

A Personal Encounter Beneath the Stars

Several years ago, I stood beneath a vast, star-filled sky in the crisp mountain air of France. Gazing upward at countless shimmering stars, I felt both incredibly small and wonderfully known. In that moment,

God's gentle whisper reached my heart clearly: "I created all *this*, *and* I created and deeply love you."

Instantly, heaven didn't feel distant—it felt remarkably near and profoundly personal.

Franklin reflected with gratitude, "Thank You, Abba Father, for Your immensity—and yet Your care in every tiny detail of creation."

Heaven Meets Your Everyday Life

When Paul described someone being "caught up to the third heaven" (2 Cor. 12:2), he emphasized that heaven isn't merely "up there"—it intersects your everyday life through prayer. Right now you have direct access to heaven's limitless resources:

- **Peace** amid conflict
- **Wisdom** in confusion
- **Strength** in weakness
- Divine **provision** in need

God transcends the infinitely vast and the infinitely small. He holds galaxies in His hands—and He draws near to the brokenhearted (see Ps. 34:18).

> The heavens declare the glory of God;
> the skies proclaim the work of His hands. (Ps. 19:1)

James discovered, "Understanding that my prayers reach heaven taught me to pray boldly. I now approach my Father confidently, trusting He is greater than every challenge I face."

Practical Steps to Lift Your Eyes

- **Simple Visualization:** Picture your prayers rising directly to heaven, reaching your attentive Father.
- **Heavenly Reminder:** Throughout the day, whisper, "My Father in heaven sees me, hears me, and deeply cares for me right now."

Reflection Question

- How might your everyday life change if you fully embraced the truth that your Father in heaven tenderly watches over every moment?

Let's Pray Together

Heavenly Father,

Creator of galaxies yet tender Father of my heart, I lift my eyes to You.

The starry heavens were humanity's first cathedral, teaching us awe and worship. As I pray, heaven doesn't remain distant—it fills my heart with Your presence.

Beneath Your vast heavens, I feel sheltered by Your loving reign. Today, help me fully open my heart to Your heavenly perspective.

Transform my worries into worship, my fears into faith, and every challenge into an opportunity for Your grace.

Draw me closer each day, until heaven's light fills every corner of my life.

In Jesus' inviting and powerful name, amen.

Where We Go from Here

Now, with our hearts firmly anchored in heaven, we're ready to move forward to honor and reverence His holy name.

In the next chapter, we'll step deeper into the wonder and beauty of declaring "Hallowed be Your name."

Are you ready to journey further into His sacred presence?

Take a deeper dive into this chapter by listening to this podcast episode:

https://ericcelerier.net/podcast-11

Chapter 12

Holy Ground

"Hallowed be your name."

Matthew 6:9

We now step into the first sacred room on the upper floor of our spiritual house—a room fully dedicated to heaven's reality. Here, no windows are necessary because the Father's presence illuminates every corner.

Understanding Holiness

In the original Greek, the word translated "hallowed" is *hagiasthētō*, meaning to set apart as holy. In fact, in the Greek text, "holy" is placed first for emphasis. When we say, "Hallowed be your name" we aren't asking God to become holy—He already is infinitely holy. Rather, we're praying that His holiness be recognized, honored, and revealed clearly on earth just as it is in heaven.

This distinction is crucial. We're not praying for God to change but for ourselves and the world around us to align with His holy nature.

The Curtain Torn: Access Granted

In the Jerusalem temple, a heavy curtain separated the Most Holy Place from the people. Only the high priest could enter once a year—and even then, only after elaborate rituals. But when Jesus died, something incredible happened:

> The curtain of the temple was torn in two from top to bottom. (Mark 15:38)

The tearing was from top to bottom, signifying divine initiative. Through Christ, every believer now enjoys direct, continual access to the holy presence of God.

> Since we have confidence to enter the Most Holy Place by the blood of Jesus,... let us draw near to God with a sincere heart. (Heb. 10:19, 22)

Holy Fire That Purifies

God's holiness is often depicted as fire—but it's not destructive; it's refining.

> [Our] God is a consuming fire. (Heb. 12:29)

His holiness burns away impurities, leaving our hearts purified and warmed by His presence.

> As Liam shared, "God's holy fire doesn't burn His children—it gently burns away impurities left by the enemy. Now I approach God freely, knowing I'm made holy by Jesus."

Join the Heavenly Chorus

At this very moment, angels proclaim in heaven:

> "Holy, holy, holy
> is the Lord God Almighty,"
> who was, and is, and is to come. (Rev. 4:8)

When you pray "Hallowed be your name," you join this eternal song, declaring His perfect love, purity, mercy, and compassion.

A Personal Encounter with Holiness

One quiet morning, as soft sunlight filled the room where I was praying, an unexpected sense of God's holiness enveloped me—not overwhelming or intimidating but deeply comforting. It was as if God Himself stepped gently into the room, surrounding me with peace. From that day forward, a clearer awareness of His holiness began shaping my daily thoughts and prayers.

> Paige expressed it like this, "Even when my life feels messy, God's holiness invites me closer. He meets me right in my brokenness, not my perfection."

Practical Steps into Holiness

- **Take a Sacred Pause:** Pause right now. Take a deep breath. Acknowledge that you're in the presence of a holy God.
- **Speak the Angels' Song:** "Holy, holy, holy is the Lord God Almighty." Feel yourself joining heaven's ongoing worship.
- **Invite His Refining Fire:** Quietly ask God to gently purify your heart and thoughts by His holy fire.

Reflection Questions

- How might your interactions and decisions shift if you consciously lived each moment aware of God's holy presence?
- Which specific area of your spiritual house most needs the touch of His holiness right now?

Imagine and Visualize

Visualize your heart as a temple filling with the gentle fragrance of His presence, much like Isaiah and John saw in their heavenly visions. Let His holiness draw you closer—not in fear, but in joyful reverence.

Let's Pray Together

Holy Father,

Thank You for removing every barrier and inviting me into Your holy presence.

Today, I stand on sacred ground, fully welcomed by Your grace.

Let Your holiness gently cleanse me, illuminating what's hidden, warming what's grown cold, and breathing life where things have faded.

May every room of my heart echo heaven's praise: "Holy, holy, holy is the Lord God Almighty." Shape me daily to reflect Your holiness—not out of fear but out of deep love and gratitude.

In Jesus' holy name, amen.

Where We Go from Here

Now that we've stood on holy ground and beheld the holiness of God, it's time to pause and honor something even deeper: His name.

In the next chapter, we'll enter a room filled with reverence—where every word breathes worship: the Sacred Name.

Take a deeper dive into this chapter by listening to this podcast episode:

https://ericcelerier.net/podcast-12

Chapter 13

The Sacred Name

"Hallowed be your name."

Matthew 6:9

We now step deeper into the upper floor of our spiritual house. Here, every room radiates the gentle yet energetic glow of God's presence. No windows are needed, for His glory fills every corner. In this sacred place, we pause to honor His name—the essential starting point of authentic prayer.

The Weight and Wonder of the Name

In Hebrew tradition, God's name—YHWH, the sacred Tetragrammaton—was considered so holy that scribes washed their hands and even changed pens before writing it. They avoided pronouncing it aloud, substituting titles like Adonai (Lord).

Yet Jesus invites us to call this same God "Abba"—Father, even Daddy—drawing us into extraordinary intimacy.

When we pray "Hallowed be your name," we aren't asking God to become holy. His name is already infinitely holy. Instead, we ask for

His holiness to be acknowledged, honored, and revealed on earth, just as it is in heaven.

Marked by His Name

Throughout Scripture, God's name transforms identity and destiny. Abram became Abraham when God breathed a part of Himself into him; Sarai became Sarah (see Gen. 17:5, 15). These weren't superficial changes—they were divine.

In the same way, His holy name is written upon your heart. His breath—the Holy Spirit—marks you deeply, transforming you with divine purpose.

> Salvation is found in no one else, for there is no other name under heaven given to mankind by which we must be saved. (Acts 4:12)

The Beauty and Richness of God's Name

Scripture overflows with vibrant names revealing the depth of God's character:

- **Elohim**—creator of all
- **Yahweh**—the great I AM
- **El Shaddai**—Almighty One
- **Jehovah Jireh**—our provider
- **Jehovah Rapha**—our healer
- **Jehovah Nissi**—our banner
- **Jehovah Shalom**—our peace

- **Jehovah Rohi**—our shepherd
- **Jehovah Tsidkenu**—our righteousness

Over a hundred names and titles fill Scripture, each inviting us deeper into God's majesty, closeness, and love.

Declaration of His Name

Let's join the heavens and declare:

> Your name is great!
> Your name is glorious!
> Your name is perfect!
> Your name is wonderful!
> Your name is incomparable!
> Your name is the fire that purifies, the rock that anchors,
> the river that refreshes!
> Your name is worthy of praise!
> Your name echoes across every nation, every language,
> every generation!

> From the rising of the sun to the place where it sets,
> the name of the LORD is to be praised. (Ps. 113:3)

Personal Reflection: His Name on My Heart

I vividly remember a special moment in Jerusalem, kneeling at the garden tomb. Feeling the coolness of the stone beneath my knees and a gentle breeze in the olive trees, I sensed God's name deeply etched into my heart, bringing extraordinary peace and clarity.

Anne Marie once told me, "Even when my mind cannot grasp the immensity of YHWH, I command my soul to praise and glorify Him. His holiness turns my heart into a sacred meeting place."

Practical Steps to Honor His Name

- **Whisper His Name with Awe:** Pause and softly say, "Holy, holy, holy is the Lord God Almighty." Let this simple act remind you of His closeness and greatness.
- **Reflect on His Names:** Today choose one name of God (like Jehovah Jireh or El Shaddai) and meditate on it throughout the day.
- **Bless His Name:** Take brief moments throughout your day to pray, "Bless the Lord, O my soul; and all that is within me, bless His holy name!" (Ps. 103:1 NKJV)

Reflection Questions

- How would your prayers transform if you truly grasped the sacredness and power of God's name?
- In what area do you most need to honor His name today?

Let's Pray Together

Holy Father,

Thank You for the privilege of calling on Your sacred name. From Abraham until today, Your name has shaped destinies, transformed lives, and demonstrated Your everlasting faithfulness.

Write Your name deeply on my heart, shaping my thoughts, words, and actions. Help me live a life that honors Your holiness, compassion, and majesty.

Let my house of prayer become an altar where Your name is joyfully celebrated from sunrise to sunset. Fill my soul with the awe that moves angels and saints to cry: "Holy, holy, holy is the Lord God Almighty, who was, and is, and is to come!"

Today, I choose to lift Your name above all else. I believe that everything I ask in Your name carries the authority of heaven, as Jesus promised.

You are the Alpha and the Omega, the Beginning and End, Everlasting Father and Prince of Peace.

I honor You. I bless You. I magnify Your holy name.

In Jesus' holy and powerful and sacred name, amen.

Where We Go from Here

Having embraced the sacredness of God's name, we now prepare our hearts for His kingdom to come.

Are you ready to welcome His reign more deeply into your spiritual house?

Take a deeper dive into this chapter by listening to this podcast episode:

https://ericcelerier.net/podcast-13

Chapter 14

Your Kingdom Come

"Your kingdom come."

Matthew 6:10

We are now stepping into the central room on the upper floor of our house of prayer. Its position is intentional, as the kingdom of God occupies a central place throughout the Bible and in our spiritual journeys. Here, we consciously invite and seek the fullness of God's kingdom over every part of our lives.

The Heartbeat of Jesus' Mission

The kingdom was at the very heart of Jesus' message. It is mentioned over a hundred times in the Gospels—far more frequently than the word *church*. While the church is vital, described as "the pillar and foundation of the truth" (1 Tim. 3:15), the kingdom is even greater. It represents God's perfect reign of justice, mercy, healing, and restoration.

This kingdom is not a distant hope. It's here and now—wherever God's love transforms brokenness into wholeness, despair into hope, and chaos into peace.

Jesus said:

> Seek first his kingdom and his righteousness, and all these things will be given to you as well. (Matt. 6:33)

A Royal Story Unfolding

Originally, humanity was entrusted with the stewardship over creation (see Gen. 1:28), called to reflect God's rule on earth. Sin disrupted this divine design, yet God's mercy persisted.

Initially, Israel had no king and was guided by judges. But without clear leadership, "everyone did what was right in his own eyes" (Judg. 17:6 NKJV). Eventually, God raised up David—a king after His own heart—as a foreshadowing of the true and eternal King: Jesus.

The angel Gabriel told Mary:

> The Lord God will give Him the throne of His father David, and he will reign over Jacob's descendants forever; his kingdom will never end. (Luke 1:32–33)

And Revelation confirms that one day, the whole earth will acknowledge:

> The kingdom of the world has become
> the kingdom of our Lord and of his Messiah,
> and he will reign for ever and ever. (11:15)

Jesus is King! He is the King of Kings.

The Struggle and Surrender: A Personal Turning Point

On June 17, 2018, my wife Muriel and I found ourselves on a crowded train in France during yet another rail strike. Over several months, we'd been wrestling deeply with a pressing question: Whose kingdom were we really building—ours or His?

To gain clarity, I proposed a unique exercise to Muriel: We often advised others, so if we were to counsel Eric and Muriel Célérier, what would we say to ourselves?

As Muriel took notes, a remarkable sense of God's presence filled that packed train carriage, transforming it into a sacred place, outside of ordinary space and time. We heard the Holy Spirit speak clearly: "Give it all to Me. Pass it on to others. If you hold on to what you have, I can only add. But if you surrender it fully, I will multiply it—not for your glory, but for My kingdom."

God even gave me a clear multiplication formula:

> What you give × faith × humility × empowering others
> = exponential multiplication for My kingdom.
> What you keep = addition for yourself.

We chose surrender. It wasn't easy—in fact, it was startlingly painful. Months of mourning, deep questioning, and wrestling followed. Yet through this surrender, something remarkable began unfolding: new horizons emerged, unexpected doors opened, and God accelerated the advance of His kingdom in ways we'd never imagined.

This book itself is proof of that surrender! I never imagined becoming a published author in English or Spanish. Yet here you are, reading these words—another beautiful testimony to how surrender unleashes God's exponential multiplication. I also never dreamed of becoming the first global ambassador for *The Chosen*, privileged to witness firsthand a true multiplication for God's kingdom

Carrying God's Presence into Every Area of Your Life

Picture each area of your life as a room needing the King's loving reign:

- **Family and Relationships:** Offer forgiveness, patience, kindness.
- **Work and Ambitions:** Serve with integrity, compassion, and excellence.
- **Finances and Stewardship:** Use resources wisely and generously.
- **Emotional and Mental Health:** Transform anxieties into prayers, trusting His peace.
- **Dreams and Desires:** Surrender ambitions, aligning them with His greater purposes.

As Martina once expressed, "May His kingdom come truly within me, radiating through me, for the good of everyone He places on my path."

Practical Steps to Embrace His Kingdom

- **Today's Invitation:** Identify one area of your life where you still cling to control. Right now, surrender it to King Jesus in prayer.
- **Reflect and Realign:** Before you sleep, ask yourself, "Did I live today seeking first the kingdom?"

Reflection Question

- What personal "kingdom"—what dream, fear, or ambition—do you need to surrender today so His kingdom can reign more fully?

Let's Pray Together

Heavenly Father,

Today, I joyfully invite Your kingdom into every room of my spiritual house. Transform my heart, guide my choices, and shape each relationship according to Your perfect and loving reign.

Tear down any small kingdoms I have built for myself. Replace them with Your glorious kingdom of light, love, peace, and truth.

Help me surrender daily, exchanging my desires for Your eternal purposes. To pray "Your kingdom come" is to surrender the kingdom of self and enthrone Christ alone. Only hearts that mirror the King's heart can truly carry His kingdom into the world.

Make my life a vibrant house of prayer, filled constantly with Your presence and peace. Every time Your kingdom advances within me, the kingdom of darkness retreats.

You are the King of Kings, and Your kingdom will never end. Come reign fully in me.

In the powerful and compassionate name of Jesus, amen.

Where We Go from Here

With hearts fully surrendered to His kingdom, we are now ready to journey into the next room: "Your will be done."

Are you ready to align your dreams and decisions with His perfect will?

Take a deeper dive into this chapter by listening to this podcast episode:

https://ericcelerier.net
/podcast-14

Chapter 15

Your Will Be Done

"Your will be done."

Matthew 6:10

Having honored God's holy name and welcomed His kingdom, we now step into the third room on the upper floor of our house of prayer—a room fully devoted to surrendering our lives to God's perfect will.

Embracing God's Perfect Authority

The Bible opens with profound simplicity:

> In the beginning God created the heavens and the earth. (Gen. 1:1)

In Hebrew, the word used for God is Elohim, a plural form indicating majesty and, as many Christians believe, hinting at the Trinity: Father, Son, and Holy Spirit. From the very first verse, we see God's perfect will clearly expressed: He speaks, and creation responds.

> God said, "Let there be light," and there was light. (Gen. 1:3)

When we pray "Your will be done," we align ourselves with this creative, sovereign God who brings beauty and order out of chaos. His will is never burdensome—it is always the joyful design of a loving Father.

> As Camila reflected, "Even in painful moments, when I surrendered to God's redirection, I later realized it was exactly right—even when it hurt."

Bridging Heaven and Earth

God intended earth to mirror heaven's harmony. Humanity, fashioned from the dust yet animated by God's Spirit, was designed to live under His loving will. Obedience wasn't meant to enslave—it was meant to bring freedom and intimacy.

Adam's disobedience shattered that unity. Now every time we pray "Your will be done, on earth as it is in heaven," we invite God to restore that broken relationship and bring His perfect order back into our lives.

Disobedience caused humanity's fall; obedience paves the way for heaven's restoration.

Discerning and Embracing His Will

God reveals His will primarily through two complementary pathways:

- **Logos:** His eternal, unchanging Word—Jesus Himself and the Scriptures.
- **Rhema:** His timely, personal word—specific promptings given by the Holy Spirit.

For example, Logos gives general guidance:

> Love your neighbor as yourself. (Matt. 22:39)

But Rhema personalizes this:

> *Today, love specifically that difficult coworker with patience and kindness.*

Paul reminds us:

> Do not conform to the pattern of this world, but be transformed by the renewing of your mind. Then you will be able to test and approve what God's will is—his good, pleasing and perfect will. (Rom. 12:2)

Annika captured this truth: "Through His Spirit and small signs, God whispers that He is near and that His will is always filled with tender love."

God's **Logos** reveals His timeless truths; His **Rhema** breathes fresh, personal guidance for our daily journey—never adding new revelation but illuminating what He has already spoken.

My Personal Journey of Surrender

Several years ago, while prayerfully walking through the serene mountains of Colorado, I sensed the Holy Spirit whisper, "Write the vision."

Writing wasn't part of my plan. Yet surrendering to that Rhema word opened doors I could never have imagined: devotionals touching lives across continents, and now this book—a living testimony of what happens when we say, "Your will be done."

> Lillian shared similarly, "I prayed for a promotion for years. Instead, I lost my job. But God led me to a far better place, unfolding His plans beyond my greatest hopes."

The Battle between Kingdoms

Praying "Your will be done" declares war against both the kingdom of self and the kingdom of darkness. Lucifer's rebellion was the first act of disobedience in heaven. Each act of your obedience brings heaven's reality closer to earth.

Choosing God's will often involves internal wrestling—moments of tears, uncertainty, even grief. Yet each surrender, though difficult, is deeply transformative and freeing.

Each time you choose surrender over self-will, humility over pride, trust over fear, heaven's influence grows stronger within you.

Practical Steps to Embrace God's Will

- **Today's Act of Trust:** Think of one area where you resist God's will. Right now, release it into His hands with confidence.
- **Logos and Rhema Reflection:** Choose one Scripture today. Ask God to breathe fresh Rhema light into it, revealing new dimensions for your life.

Reflection Question

- Where is God inviting you today to trust His will more deeply—and what would genuine surrender look like in that place?

Let's Pray Together

Heavenly Father,

Today I lay down my ambitions, fears, and dreams before You. I choose Your will above mine.

Father, gently tear down the small kingdoms I've pridefully built for myself. Replace them with Your kingdom.

Renew my mind through Your eternal Word (Logos). Guide my steps clearly through Your personal word (Rhema). Transform my spiritual house of prayer into a sanctuary where heaven's will always reigns.

Give me the courage and strength to obey, even when it feels difficult. Help me trust fully that Your will is always better, wiser, and overflowing with love.

I echo Jesus' prayer: "Here I am … I have come to do your will, my God" (Heb. 10:7).

In Jesus' powerful and compassionate name, amen.

Where We Go from Here

Having surrendered fully to the Father's perfect will, we now step into the sacred threshold connecting heaven and earth.

In the next chapter, we'll pause at the spiritual staircase—the place where heaven begins to descend directly into our daily lives. Here, our prayer shifts from God's realm to our everyday needs.

Are you ready to receive everything heaven longs to bring into your life today?

Take a deeper dive into this chapter by listening to this podcast episode:

https://ericcelerier.net/podcast-15

Reflection and Prayer

Reflection and Prayer

Part 3

WHERE HEAVEN TOUCHES EARTH

Chapter 16

On Earth as It Is in Heaven

"On earth as it is in heaven."

Matthew 6:10

Having fully explored the "upper floor" of our spiritual house—intimacy with Abba, reverence for His holy name, the coming of His kingdom, and surrender to His perfect will—we now step onto a sacred staircase. This staircase symbolizes the heart of the Lord's Prayer: the profound mystery where heaven touches earth.

When Muriel and I surrendered our lives completely to God's will—giving away our ministry, influence, and even our dreams—we experienced firsthand what it truly means for heaven to descend. Our surrender opened floodgates we didn't even know existed, releasing an abundance we could never have imagined. It was exactly this kind of sacred moment Jesus describes: when heaven visibly breaks into the ordinary moments of our lives.

Heaven Descending: More Than a Prayer

In the original Greek, the first three petitions of the Lord's Prayer form a captivating rhythm:

- *Hagiasthētō to onoma sou* (May Your name be sanctified)
- *Elthētō hē basileia sou* (May Your kingdom come)
- *Genēthētō to thelēma sou* (May Your will be done)

Each phrase emphasizes *sou* ("your"), building momentum until we reach the pivotal phrase:

- *Hōs en ouranō kai epi tēs gēs* (On earth as it is in heaven)

This poetic structure reveals something weighty. "On earth as it is in heaven" isn't just about God's will—it applies equally to His name being honored, His kingdom coming, and His will being fully embraced in our everyday lives.

Prayer, then, isn't merely lifting requests toward heaven; it's opening our hearts and lives for heaven's realities to flow downward.

Heaven's Reality in Everyday Life

Imagine a difficult relationship. Human instincts push toward defensiveness or bitterness. But when heaven descends, defensiveness melts into humility, bitterness transforms into forgiveness, and divine love reshapes our reactions.

Picture your workplace: See it not simply as a place of routine tasks but as a mission field where heaven's creativity, integrity, and wisdom can flourish and inspire every interaction.

> Paige shared, "The true revelation isn't about trying to reach heaven but about inviting heaven to earth through our lives. It's incredible that God wants to partner with us in this way!"

Personal Encounter: HelloBible and Heaven's Touch

Recently, while developing the app HelloBible, I faced overwhelming complexity. One evening, as frustration mounted, the Holy Spirit gently whispered, "Eric, you're not building this alone. Invite heaven into every decision, every line of code, every feature."

That night, my workspace transformed from ordinary to extraordinary—solutions emerged effortlessly, creativity flowed freely, and clarity illuminated every step. It was an unforgettable reminder: when we intentionally invite heaven's realities, even the most ordinary spaces become sacred.

Practical Steps to Bring Heaven Closer

- **Today's Invitation:** Pause and reflect right now—what area of your life feels disconnected from heaven's peace? Take a moment and invite God's presence specifically into that situation.

- **Simple Action:** In your next conversation, consciously reflect heaven's kindness, patience, or truth.

Reflection Question

- If you truly believed heaven's realities were accessible right now, what would you approach differently in your daily life?

Let's Pray Together

Heavenly Father,

Thank You that heaven isn't distant or inaccessible. Today I conciously open every area of my life to You. Replace my anxieties with Your peace. Guide my confusion with Your wisdom. Let Your divine love shape every interaction.

Transform my life into a visible bridge between heaven and earth. Let my home become a sanctuary, my workplace a mission field, and my heart an altar of Your presence. I want my everyday life to show the world that heaven is already breaking in, here and now.

In Jesus' powerful name, amen.

Where We Go from Here

You've just prayed one of the most daring lines in all of Scripture: "On earth as it is in heaven."

Take a deeper dive into this chapter by listening to this podcast episode:
https://ericcelerier.net/podcast-16

This is not a poetic ideal. It's a call to surrender your plans, your pace, and even your expectations—so that God's will, not yours, becomes the center.

But how do we live that out? How do we carry heaven into our workplaces, families, and quiet moments?

Before we move on to asking, we must go deeper into abiding.

In the next chapter, we'll rise again—into the space where adoration becomes atmosphere and God's presence reorders everything.

Chapter 17

As in Heaven

"On earth as it is in heaven."

Matthew 6:10

Having ascended the upper floors of our spiritual house—where we experienced intimacy with Abba, honored His holy name, welcomed His kingdom, and surrendered to His perfect will—we now enter the sacred corridor where heaven touches earth. This is not merely a transition—it is the heart of the Lord's Prayer, where heaven descends to meet daily life.

Yet let's be honest. Experiencing heaven's reality in our daily lives isn't always easy. Sometimes it feels elusive, almost out of reach. But Jesus taught us this prayer precisely because He knew we'd struggle to bridge these two worlds

Heaven First, Earth Second

The original Greek emphasizes heaven first: *Hōs en ouranō kai epi tēs gēs*, meaning, "as in heaven, so also on earth."

From the Bible's very first verse, "In the beginning God created the heavens and the earth" (Gen. 1:1), heaven precedes earth. God's design is clear: what is established above is meant to overflow below.

Jesus confirmed this heavenly priority:

> Seek first his kingdom and his righteousness, and all these things will be given to you as well. (Matt. 6:33)

Our prayers aren't just cries lifted upward. They are bold invitations for heaven's blessings to rush downward into our daily lives.

Jacob's Ladder: The Gateway of Heaven

When in Bethel, Jacob dreamed of a ladder connecting earth and heaven, with angels ascending and descending (see Gen. 28:10–17). Awaking in awe, he declared:

> Surely the LORD is in this place.... How awesome is this place! This is none other than the house of God; this is the gate of heaven." (vv. 16–17)

This dream foreshadowed Jesus:

> Very truly I tell you, you will see "heaven open, and the angels of God ascending and descending on" the Son of Man. (John 1:51)

Through Christ, your heart becomes a living Bethel—a gate where heaven's wonders flow onto the earth.

Declare it over your life:

> **This is the house of God; this is the gate of heaven!**

Melchizedek's Blessing: Heavenly Provision

In Israel, Muriel and I stood on an archaeological site believed to be linked to Melchizedek, priest-king of Salem. Long before Solomon's temple, blessings were spoken and heaven's abundance poured out.

Melchizedek blessed Abram:

> Blessed be Abram by God Most High,
> Creator of heaven and earth. (Gen. 14:19)

Abram responded by offering a tithe, acknowledging heaven's priority over earthly possessions. Heaven first—earth blessed second.

> Payton shared, "When I realize the kingdom of heaven is within me, my house becomes a gate of heaven—a place where blessings descend and radiate outward."

Living with Heaven's Priorities

When heaven descends:

- In relationships, forgiveness overtakes resentment.
- In workplaces, creativity and integrity flourish.
- In emotions, peace overwhelms anxiety.
- In finances, generosity replaces fear.

A. W. Tozer's understanding of this concept is often expressed like this:

> As God is exalted to the right place in our lives, a thousand problems are solved all at once.

Heaven's descent is not a distant dream—it's a daily reality for every surrendered heart.

Practical Steps to Living "As in Heaven"

- **Today's Visualization:** Picture heaven's gifts cascading into your home, work, and relationships.
- **Immediate Action:** Choose one specific situation today and consciously invite heaven's peace, wisdom, or joy to reign.

Reflection Question

- Where is God inviting you to become a living gateway for heaven to flood into earth?

Let's Pray Together

Heavenly Father,

Today, I boldly proclaim, "This is the house of God; this is the gate of heaven!"

Let Your peace invade my chaos.

Let Your wisdom illuminate my confusion.

Let Your abundance flood my emptiness.

I open wide the doors of my heart, my home, my work, and my relationships.

Let heaven descend boldly through me.

Make my life a living bridge where Your kingdom reigns, Your name is glorified, and Your will is joyfully fulfilled.

Let angels ascend and descend over the ladder of Your promises in my life.

Let every corner of my house of prayer echo heaven's song of hope.

Heaven's arrival is not theory—it is reality. Let it live, breathe, and flow through me today.

In Jesus' name, amen.

William reflected, "The Lord's Prayer is structured like a divine descent: first heaven, then God's name, His kingdom, His will—and finally earth. Every prayer can open a gate for heaven's reality."

Where We Go from Here

Now that we've stood in the sacred corridor where heaven rushes into earth, the question becomes: How do we access this divine exchange personally and daily?

In the next chapter, we'll step through the only true doorway into this heavenly reality—**Jesus Himself**. He is not just the one who teaches us to pray—**He is the gate** through which every heavenly promise enters our lives.

Take a deeper dive into this chapter by listening to this podcast episode:

https://ericcelerier.net/podcast-17

Chapter 18

The Gate of Heaven

"I am the gate; whoever enters through me will be saved. They will come in and go out, and find pasture."

John 10:9

As we move from the heavenly upper floors of our spiritual house into the daily realities on the ground level, we encounter a gate clearly marked with these profound words: "**I am the gate.**"

This gate isn't merely an entrance—it's **Jesus Himself**, the living, breathing connection between eternity and everyday life. He makes the divine accessible and intimately present in every aspect of our lives.

Only through Jesus

When Jesus declared, "No one comes to the Father except through me" (John 14:6), He wasn't being exclusive—He was being clear. Jesus alone bridges heaven and earth, giving our prayers true power and transforming ordinary moments into divine encounters.

Every prayer offered through Christ connects us deeply and personally with our heavenly Father.

Jesus Revealed in the Lord's Prayer

Every phrase of the Lord's Prayer reveals Jesus' identity.

- **"Our Father in heaven":** Jesus descended from heaven to show us that He and the Father are one.
- **"Hallowed be your name":** Jesus embodies holiness—the name above all names, Emmanuel—God with us.
- **"Your kingdom come":** Jesus is the King who establishes God's kingdom on earth.
- **"Your will be done, on earth as it is in heaven":** Jesus perfectly fulfilled the Father's will, even unto the cross.
- **"Give us today our daily bread":** Jesus, born in Bethlehem (the "House of Bread"), is the Bread of Life.
- **"And forgive us our debts, as we also have forgiven our debtors":** Jesus provides ultimate forgiveness.
- **"And lead us not into temptation, but deliver us from the evil one":** Jesus overcame temptation and defeated evil.
- **"For yours is the kingdom and the power and the glory forever":** Jesus reigns with eternal authority and glory.[1]
- **"Amen":** Jesus' word is truth.

Understanding this transforms the Lord's Prayer: it's not merely a prayer taught by Jesus—it's a prayer that **reveals Jesus**.

He is the living key unlocking every room in our spiritual house.

> Parker reflected, "My longing is for Jesus to feed me daily—not just physically but spiritually, emotionally, and mentally, so that I may carry His life everywhere."

The Gate as Our Daily Reality

Recognizing Jesus as the gate impacts every aspect of our lives:

- **Decisions** are guided by His wisdom.
- **Relationships** thrive on His grace.
- **Challenges** yield to His peace.
- **Weaknesses** become platforms for His strength.

Jesus promises: "They will come in and go out, and find pasture" (John 10:9).

Through Him, we don't just find initial salvation—we find daily nourishment, security, freedom, and abundant life.

Connecting Heaven to Your Heart

C. S. Lewis insightfully wrote:

> Aim at heaven and you will get earth "thrown in": aim at earth and you get neither.[2]

Every time you consciously enter through Jesus, your heart becomes a living gateway where heaven touches earth.

> Aurora testified, "Through years of healing from injustice and pain, it was Jesus—the Prince of Peace—who guided me gently through the gate into freedom and lasting joy.

Practical Steps to Enter through Jesus

- **Start with Jesus:** Today, begin your prayer by explicitly stating, "Father, I come to You through Jesus, my gateway."
- **Heavenly Visualization:** Picture yourself stepping through Jesus into the Father's embrace, receiving grace, wisdom, and peace.
- **Intentional Commitment:** Identify a current challenge. Place it willingly in the hands of Jesus, your gate.

Reflection Question

- Where is Jesus inviting you today to step through Him into greater peace, strength, or provision?

Let's Pray Together

Lord Jesus,

You are the gate. You are the way, the truth, and the life. Today, I step through You into the Father's presence.

I lay down my fears, my burdens, and my ambitions at Your feet.

Feed me with Your life. Strengthen me with Your wisdom. Guide me with Your peace.

Transform my ordinary moments into extraordinary encounters where heaven meets earth.

Let my life be a living house of prayer, where every door is opened by You and through You.

Thank You for being the door, the Shepherd, the Savior, and the Lord. I embrace You as my gateway to the Father's heart.

In Your powerful and loving name, amen.

Where We Go from Here

Having stepped through the gate and encountered Jesus afresh, we're now ready to deepen our spiritual sight. In the next chapter, we'll explore how authentic repentance clears our hearts to see Him more clearly.

Are you ready to walk deeper into intimacy?

Take a deeper dive into this chapter by listening to this podcast episode:

https://ericcelerier.net/podcast-18

Chapter 19

Seeing Jesus through Repentance

"When he comes, he will prove the world to be in the wrong about sin and righteousness and judgment."
John 16:8

As we've walked through the rooms of the house of prayer, drawing closer to the Father—calling Him Abba, hallowing His name, seeking His kingdom, and surrendering to His will—we now enter a quieter, often overlooked room: **repentance**.

But here, something extraordinary happens. In this room, we begin to see Jesus not as an idea but as a living presence. And through the gentle guidance of the Holy Spirit, we are drawn back into deep communion with the Father

Repentance as a Spiritual X-Ray

In the world of art, the term *repentir* describes when painters like Leonardo da Vinci, Van Gogh, and Picasso altered their work—painting over earlier versions. These hidden layers are invisible to the naked eye, but with X-ray technology, they come to light.

Repentance functions similarly in our souls. It's not just saying we're sorry; it's allowing the Holy Spirit to reveal the hidden layers—motivations, wounds, pride, and fears—that blur our view of Jesus.

The beauty of repentance is not in the shame it exposes but in the clarity it brings. It's the sacred moment when the fog lifts and Jesus steps fully into view.

Seeing Jesus' Gifts to Us in Every Phrase

Genuine repentance does more than cleanse us; it sharpens our vision. Suddenly, in the Lord's Prayer, we see the work that Jesus, our redeemer, does for us:

- **"Our Father in heaven"**—Jesus brings us into the Father's embrace (see Rom. 8:15).
- **"Hallowed be your Name"**—Jesus reveals a holy God we can know personally (see John 17:6).
- **"Your kingdom come"**—Jesus is the king who brings heaven near to us (see Luke 17:21).
- **"Your will be done, on earth as it is in heaven"**—Jesus obeyed the Father's will perfectly, opening heaven's door for us (see Phil. 2:8).
- **"Give us today our daily bread"**—Jesus is the Bread of Life, who sustains us (see John 6:35).
- **"And forgive us our debts, as we also have forgiven our debtors"**—Jesus forgave from the cross and teaches us to forgive (see Luke 23:34).

- **"And lead us not into temptation"**—Jesus overcame temptation and strengthens us (see 1 Cor. 10:13).
- **"But deliver us from the evil one"**—Jesus conquered evil on our behalf (see Col. 2:15).
- **"For yours is the kingdom and the power and the glory forever. Amen."**—Jesus reigns with eternal glory and welcomes us (see Rev. 5:12–13).

Repentance isn't about groveling—it's about refocusing. And when we refocus, Jesus steps into view, and the Father's heart shines more clearly through Him.

Lisa shared, "Repentance showed me clearly how deeply my actions had hurt others. Seeing Jesus' mercy so clearly made me treasure His grace at my deepest level."

The Holy Spirit: Our Gentle Guide

The Holy Spirit never condemns us in repentance; He lovingly lifts the layers from our hearts.

He is the Architect behind the Lord's Prayer, inspiring every word to reveal the Son and lead us back to the Father.

As Max Lucado said with candor and grace:

> God loves you just the way you are, but he refuses to leave you there. He wants you to be just like Jesus.[1]

Repentance is how the Spirit gently shapes us into Christ's likeness.

A Challenge to You

Have your prayers felt foggy lately? Maybe you've been overwhelmed by responsibilities, stretched thin by life, or quietly carrying the weight of pride or self-reliance.

What if the one thing standing between you and renewed clarity is simply ... repentance?

When you stop and confess—honestly, humbly, wholeheartedly—Jesus doesn't withdraw. The Holy Spirit whispers, and heaven's light floods in.

This isn't theory. This is transformation. And it's available today.

Abigail reflected, "Each step of repentance deepened my intimacy with Christ. His grace lifted my guilt and flooded my heart with joy."

Practical Applications

- **Daily Action:** As you pray the Lord's Prayer, pause after each line and simply whisper, "Jesus, show Yourself to me here."
- **Reflective Question:** What area of your life feels foggy right now? What step of repentance might bring clarity?

The Spiritual and Emotional Gifts of Repentance

Repentance doesn't lead to heaviness—it leads to lightness. When Jesus becomes visible again, you experience:

- Deeper intimacy with God
- Lasting peace replacing guilt
- A more authentic, joyful prayer life
- A heart continually reshaped by love

Theological Insight

Repentance is not a detour in the Christian life—it's the way forward.

In the ancient Shema, God's people were called to love Him fully—and to return again and again whenever they wandered. Repentance is returning to love.

Let's Pray Together

Heavenly Father,

Thank You that repentance is not condemnation but invitation. It's the space where I see Jesus again.

Holy Spirit, lead me lovingly into the light. Reveal what needs healing, not to shame me but to restore me.

Let repentance be my daily bridge back into Your loving arms. Let every prayer be clearer, deeper, and more alive with Your presence.

Today, I step into Your light again. I come home.

In Jesus' name, amen.

Where We Go from Here

Now that the fog has lifted and Jesus stands clearly before us, we're ready to ascend further.

In the next chapter, we'll explore how love rises from our hearts—and how heaven's grace rushes down to meet us.

Are you ready to take the next step?

Take a deeper dive into this chapter by listening to this podcast episode:

https://ericcelerier.net/podcast-19

Chapter 20

The Stairs

"Every good and perfect gift is from above, coming down from the Father of the heavenly lights."

James 1:17

In a multilevel house, stairs connect the different floors. They enable movement, create access, and make transitions possible. In your spiritual house of prayer, the stairs represent something even greater—a holy rhythm, a dynamic relationship between your heart and heaven. Your prayers rise. God's grace descends. Your worship ascends. His peace pours out.

Just like Jacob, who dreamed of angels ascending and descending a ladder from heaven (see Gen. 28:12), we are invited to see our spiritual lives as deeply connected to heaven. Nothing is static. Everything flows through this divine staircase.

I remember visiting the Burj Khalifa in Dubai—the tallest tower in the world—with Muriel. We were amazed that it only took a minute to reach the observation deck. What would take hours on foot became instant. I thought: *This is prayer. The connection between our heavenly Father and us is immediate. The moment we say, "Our Father in heaven," the staircase of grace is already in motion.*

And yet ... sometimes the answers seem to take the stairs instead of the elevator.

Jesus, the True Staircase

Jesus declared, "You will see 'heaven open, and the angels of God ascending and descending on' the Son of Man" (John 1:51).

He is not just our Savior—He is the staircase itself. The connection point. The bridge. Fully God, fully human, He links your ordinary life to extraordinary grace.

Through Him, every prayer you whisper reaches the throne room of heaven. Every gift the Father sends flows back to you through Jesus, the mediator of all grace.

A Two-Way Staircase: Love and Grace

Here's the wonder of it all: this staircase operates as a sacred double flow.

Love Ascends. The starting point is always love. "God is love" (1 John 4:16), and that love draws us upward. Think of Mary pouring perfume at Jesus' feet (see John 12:3)—her devotion rose like fragrance, filling the house. Your simple, sincere acts of love rise the same way.

Jesus reminds us, "How much more will your Father in heaven give good gifts to those who ask him!" (Matt. 7:11). His love draws your prayers upward.

Grace Descends. Grace is not just a gift; it is a river of compassion constantly flowing down. It descends not because we've earned it—but because God delights in pouring His presence into open hearts. As James wrote, "Every good and perfect gift is from above" (1:17).

Picture Queen Esther before the king. At the sight of her, he extended the golden scepter and said, "What is your request? It shall be given to you—up to half the kingdom!" (Est. 5:1–3 NKJV).

Now picture your King extending His scepter toward you. You approach a throne of grace, not of judgment.

> Hannah shared, "When I visualized prayer as ascending love and descending grace, anxiety lifted immediately. Prayer became joyful anticipation, not a burden."

A Holy Exchange in Real Time

Every time you pray, a divine exchange takes place—and it's never interrupted.

The staircase between heaven and your heart is always open, always active, always secured by Jesus. Visualize it:

- Your praise rises—His peace descends.
- Your worries rise—His wisdom descends.
- Your hunger for God rises—His Spirit satisfies.

Heaven isn't distant. It is rushing in. Even your most ordinary moment can become sacred when heaven touches earth.

A Challenge to You

Do you view prayer as a one-way message—or a sacred exchange?

What if every whisper were an invitation for grace?

You don't have to climb alone. Jesus is your staircase. Each breath, each word, each tear is carried upward—and responded to with divine care.

Grace doesn't always shout through miracles. It often whispers through mercy: peace in anxiety, strength in weakness, clarity in confusion, provision in need.

> Lisa reflected, "This sacred staircase turned my prayers into intimate encounters. Every request rose in trust, every answer descended in grace."

Practical Applications

- **Sacred Placement:** Pause now. Picture placing one burden on the staircase. Watch it rise in trust—and grace descend in return.
- **Reflective Moment:** What part of today could become a divine exchange?

Spiritual Foundations

This vision echoes the Shema:

> Love the LORD your God with all your heart and with all your soul and with all your strength. (Deut. 6:5)

Love rises. Grace descends.

As Dallas Willard remind us:

> Grace is not opposed to effort. It is opposed to earning.[1]

Grace welcomes your pursuit.

Let's Pray Together

Heavenly Father,

Thank You for Jesus, the staircase connecting my heart to Yours. Today, I offer my worship and welcome Your grace. Fill my house of prayer with the fragrance of rising devotion and descending mercy.

Let every step I take toward You be met with waves of heaven drawing near. Let prayer be my rhythm. Let grace be my foundation.

Make my life a sanctuary of ascending love and descending glory.

In Jesus' beautiful name, amen.

Where We Go from Here

Benjamin, a reader, once said: "For me, the stairs represent growth in God—an ascent toward higher places. I don't want to go back down."

Take a deeper dive into this chapter by listening to this podcast episode:

https://ericcelerier.net/podcast-20

And that's true. The stairs represent both access and ascent. In your house of prayer, they allow you to rise in worship—and descend into deeper trust, surrender, and love.

Now let's step into the first sacred room of the ground floor: "Give us today our daily bread." Heaven is about to meet your everyday life.

Reflection and Prayer

Reflection and Prayer

Part 4

THE LOWER FLOOR

Where Heaven Meets Our Needs

Chapter 21

Our Daily Bread

"Give us today our daily bread."

Matthew 6:11

As we move to the ground floor of our spiritual house of prayer, we begin to engage with our earthly needs—physical, emotional, and relational. This part of the Lord's Prayer—"Give us today our daily bread"—marks a shift from the lofty to the tangible. Here, prayer becomes incarnational. This is where our prayers touch the soil.

Jesus leads us downward, not in defeat but into dependence. Bread is where heaven meets hunger.

Bread at the Foundation

Psychologist Abraham Maslow famously placed food, water, and shelter at the base of his hierarchy of human needs. Jesus meets us there—not just to acknowledge these needs but to assure us that God cares deeply about them.

> Do not worry about your life, what you will eat or drink.... Look at the birds of the air; they do not sow or reap or store away in barns, and yet your heavenly Father feeds them. (Matt. 6:25–26)

When we ask for daily bread, we affirm: "God, You are my provider today."

Bread Dropped at the Doorstep

Years ago, when Muriel and I were young pastors, we had almost no money and a small child to care for. We prayed, "Give us today our daily bread"—sometimes quite literally. And to our amazement, food would appear on our doorstep. No note. No explanation. Just provision.

I remember opening the door to find bags of groceries or fresh produce. No one ever claimed responsibility. But we knew who had sent it: our Father in heaven.

The Mystery of *Epiousios*

The Greek word translated as "daily" is *epiousios*—a word so rare it appears only twice in Scripture. Etymologically, *epi* means "upon, above, beyond," and *ousia* means "essence, being, substance." Together, it suggests something beyond ordinary—a "supersubstantial" bread.

Saint Jerome, when translating the Gospels into Latin, used *quotidianum* ("everyday") in Luke and *supersubstantialem* ("supersubstantial") in Matthew. Jesus invites us to hold both realities together: the practical and the spiritual.

In "Origen on Prayer," the author called it "needful bread," or bread necessary for existence.[1]

N. T. Wright emphasizes throughout his work—especially about the Lord and His prayer—that the true daily bread we need is Jesus Himself, the living Word who sustains our deepest humanity.

As a dear brother said:

> The real presence of Christ is not a chemical transformation—it is a concrete encounter with the Lord who gives Himself as nourishment.

Sophia shared, "Recognizing Christ as my daily bread transformed my devotional life. Each meal now reminds me of Jesus—the living nourishment who satisfies my deepest hunger."

Jesus, the Bread of Life

Jesus proclaimed:

> I am the bread of life. Whoever comes to me will never go hungry, and whoever believes in me will never be thirsty. (John 6:35)

Born in Bethlehem—"House of Bread"—Jesus came not merely to feed crowds but to nourish souls. Saint Augustine's writings convey a similar truth: Christ is the bread of life—ever present, patiently awaiting our hunger for Him. One could summarize his thought this way: "Christ is the bread, awaiting hunger."

He waits for you today.

Communion, Presence, and Memory

At the Lord's table—whether we understand it as mystery or memorial—the bread and the cup become a meeting point of grace, memory, and presence. Across traditions, one truth remains: Christ gave Himself for us.

Bread We Share

Jesus teaches us to pray for *our* daily bread—not just my bread. This prayer roots us in community. We are called not only to receive but also to share.

In a world starving for physical and spiritual nourishment, your house of prayer must become a house of bread—a place of generosity, compassion, and provision.

Practicing the Bread of Heaven

- **Give Thanks at Meals:** Not just for the food but for Jesus, the true Bread.
- **Feed on Scripture:** Linger with the Word to fuel your soul as you would with nourishment to fuel your body.
- **Share Generously:** Find someone who hungers physically or spiritually. Ask God how you can be bread for them today.

> Marcus reflected, "Praying for daily bread became deeply meaningful once I understood the significance of *epiousios*. Now each prayer acknowledges Christ Himself sustaining my soul."

Reflection Questions

- How are you relying on Jesus as your daily supersubstance today?
- How might your house of prayer become a house of bread for others?

Let's Pray Together

Father, thank You for meeting our daily needs. Thank You even more for Jesus—the Bread of Life—who nourishes our souls and anchors our lives.

Lord Jesus, You are my supersubstantial Bread. You are my nourishment, my strength, my life. Feed me with Your Word.

Holy Spirit, awaken in me both the hunger for Christ and the joy of receiving Him. Fill me with Your Spirit. Make me mindful to share what I have received, both physically and spiritually.

Let my house of prayer be alive with the fragrance of gratitude, the taste of Your goodness, and the mission of feeding others. Let my life become a living bakery of Your Bread for a hungry world.

I receive today not just provision for my stomach but satisfaction for my soul. Thank You for being the Bread that came down from heaven to give life to the world.

In Your beautiful and nourishing name, amen.

Where We Go from Here

As we receive Christ as our daily nourishment, another hunger arises—the longing for restoration and healing.

In the next chapter, we will enter the sacred room of forgiveness, where debts are released and grace flows freely. Are you ready?

Take a deeper dive into this chapter by listening to this podcast episode:

https://ericcelerier.net/podcast-21

Chapter 22

Forgive Us Our Debts

"Forgive us our debts, as we also have forgiven our debtors."

Matthew 6:12

In our journey through the house of prayer, we've arrived at one of its most vital rooms—one dedicated entirely to forgiveness. Here lies the heart of our relationship with God and others: a place of profound freedom, reconciliation, and renewal. Forgiveness is not just another room—it's part of the foundation. Without it, the whole house risks crumbling.

Forgiveness: Our Greatest Need

When Jesus instructs us to pray "Forgive us our debts," He directs us toward a foundational truth: we all carry moral debts. In Hebrew tradition, sin was often viewed as a debt—a serious obligation toward God and others.

In fact, the Hebrew word *chov* ("debt") reflects both financial and moral obligation. In the Year of Jubilee (see Lev. 25), all debts were forgiven—a stunning foreshadowing of divine mercy.

Thus, every sin creates a spiritual debt we cannot repay. Yet Jesus lovingly invites us to receive God's total forgiveness—and to extend it.

Experiencing Forgiveness Personally

Have you ever carried a heavy burden of guilt, longing desperately for relief? Imagine the freedom of knowing that your debts have been completely wiped away by Christ's sacrifice. What changes might that bring to your relationships, your prayers, your peace?

Forgiveness isn't merely theological—it's personal. It reshapes you from the inside out.

Jesus: The Embodiment of Forgiveness

Jesus didn't just teach forgiveness; He lived it.

- John the Baptist called Him "the Lamb of God, who takes away the sin of the world" (John 1:29).
- On the cross, Jesus prayed, "Father, forgive them, for they do not know what they do" (Luke 23:34 NKJV).

Understanding Jesus as forgiveness personified transforms prayer: we don't just end prayers "in Jesus' name" formally; we enter forgiveness because of Him.

The Continuous Flow of Forgiveness

Notice the prayer says, "Forgive us ... as we also have forgiven." This shows a divine pattern:

1. We first receive God's forgiveness.
2. Then we release forgiveness to others.

Jesus illustrated this with the parable of the unforgiving servant (see Matt. 18:21–35). True forgiveness flows freely once we grasp how much we've been forgiven.

Forgiveness isn't a one-time event—it's a living river of grace that keeps our spiritual house clean from resentment and bitterness.

> Elisabeth shared, "I struggled for years with forgiving myself for my father's rejection. Then God showed me that self-forgiveness was crucial. When I finally forgave myself, overwhelming peace filled me. Forgiveness truly liberates."

A List of Common Offenses

We may not even realize how some of these have quietly settled into our hearts over time. But the Spirit does.

Consider these different areas where forgiveness may be needed:

- Indifference to others' suffering
- Harsh or judgmental thoughts
- Outbursts of anger
- Rejection or exclusion
- Lies and deceit

- Stealing or withholding
- Manipulation or control
- Abuse—emotional, verbal, or physical
- Revenge-seeking behavior
- Betrayal and broken trust
- Unwillingness to forgive

Which one touches your heart today? What might the Holy Spirit be inviting you to release?

Forgiveness doesn't minimize the hurt. It simply refuses to let hurt have the last word.

Forgiveness in Everyday Life

Forgiveness often confronts deep wounds—betrayal, rejection, harsh words. True forgiveness doesn't excuse wrongs—it hands them to Jesus, trusting His justice and mercy.

Lisa reflected, "I didn't realize how hidden resentment had poisoned my life until it almost destroyed my joy. Forgiving others—and asking for forgiveness myself—brought humbling yet meaningful healing."

The Beauty of the Word *Forgiveness*

The word "forgiveness" has intriguing roots. It comes from the Old French *pardun* and Latin *perdonare*: *per* meaning "completely," and *donare* meaning "to give." Thus, to forgive is to "give completely." Full release. Complete mercy. A gift not earned but freely offered.

To forgive is to reflect the heart of the Father—the one who gave completely through His Son.

Practical Applications

- **Daily Action:** Identify someone you need to forgive. Take one step today—pray for them, release them, or show unexpected kindness.
- **Reflective Visualization:** Picture yourself in the forgiveness room. See yourself handing each offense directly to Jesus, feeling His peace replace bitterness.
- **Letter Exercise:** Write a letter forgiving someone who hurt you. You don't need to send it—just writing it can bring tremendous healing. Even if you never send it, God will read every word.

Reflection Questions

- Who is God inviting you to forgive today?
- How would releasing that burden impact your inner peace?

Let's Pray Together

Heavenly Father,

Thank You for the immeasurable forgiveness You extend through Jesus. Today, I lay down my debts—and my grudges—at Your feet. Wash my heart clean. Fill my spirit with the freedom of Your mercy.

Empower me to forgive others as You have forgiven me. Transform my house of prayer into a sanctuary of peace, reconciliation, and grace.

Jesus, You embodied forgiveness on the cross. Help me embody it today. As I pray the prayer You taught us, may my heart mirror the mercy embedded in each line. Let every act of forgiveness become a bridge between heaven and earth.

In Your mighty and compassionate name, amen.

Where We Go from Here

Now that forgiveness has swept and cleansed this room of our spiritual house, we are ready to face the next: the room of temptation. With a heart made whole, let's learn how to stand firm in God's strength.

Take a deeper dive into this chapter by listening to this podcast episode:

https://ericcelerier.net/podcast-22

Chapter 23

Three Rooms, Three Temptations

"And lead us not into temptation."

Matthew 6:13

Having just experienced the liberating power of forgiveness, we often find ourselves vulnerable. It's in these spiritually sensitive moments, right after significant victories, that temptation tends to intensify. Now we enter the third room on the ground floor of our house of prayer—corresponding to the petition, "Lead us not into temptation."

Every temptation is ultimately a battle between our will and God's. This room teaches us to submit fully to the Father's perfect guidance, especially during times of doubt, fatigue, or spiritual vulnerability. Temptation is not abstract; it's deeply personal, emotional, and real.

Even Jesus faced it. Immediately after His baptism, when heaven opened and the Father declared, "You are My beloved Son" (Luke

3:22 NKJV), the Spirit led Jesus into the wilderness to confront temptation. Why? To show us how to resist, how to rely fully on God's strength, and how to stand secure in our identity as His beloved children.

> Michael said, "A business deal looked incredible. But the terms were unethical. Through prayer, I heard, 'Seek first My kingdom.' I walked away. God later provided in ways I never imagined."

Three Temptations, Three Rooms

Each of the temptations Jesus faced parallels a specific room in our house of prayer:

1. The First Temptation: Stones into Bread

> If You are the Son of God, command this stone to become bread. (Luke 4:3 NKJV)

The enemy attacks provision. The room of "Give us today our daily bread" becomes vulnerable when we start doubting God's goodness or feel spiritually fatigued. Jesus, secure in the Father's affirmation, responded,

> Man shall not live on bread alone, but on every word that comes from the mouth of God. (Matt. 4:4)

Many today, like the tempter suggested, seek alternative "bread"—success, approval, security—only to find emptiness. True nourishment comes from the Word of God.

2. The Second Temptation: False Kingdoms

> All this authority I will give You … if You will worship before me. (Luke 4:6–7 NKJV)

This temptation attacks our allegiance. In our spiritual house, the room where we pray "Your kingdom come" is compromised when we seek shortcuts, influence, or validation apart from God's design. Yet Jesus refused to compromise:

> Worship the Lord your God and serve him only. (v. 8)

3. The Third Temptation: Spiritual Pride

> If you are the Son of God … throw yourself down. (Matt. 4:6)

This final test was about spiritual pride—performing to impress others or forcing God to act. It corrupts the room of "Your will be done" by replacing surrender with self-importance.

But Jesus chose humble submission, answering,

> Do not put the Lord your God to the test. (v. 7)

Temptation always seeks to corrupt identity, provision, and purpose. But Jesus overcame because He knew who He was, trusted the Father's Word, and refused shortcuts. He understands the complexity and emotional weight of temptation, especially when we're weak.

> Lisa reflected, "I craved affirmation in ministry. After a painful failure, I realized I was performing more than praying. Jesus gently brought me back to quiet trust."

Final Victory Is Already Won

Temptation is real—but so is your victory.

> Submit yourselves, then, to God. Resist the devil, and he will flee from you. (James 4:7)

You don't fight alone. Christ has already triumphed. When you walk through this room with Him, you walk in power.

Practical Applications

- **Immediate Action:** Declare aloud: "I am God's beloved child. My security and provision are in Him alone."
- **Sacred Surrender:** Open your hands during prayer. Invite Jesus into those areas where you feel especially vulnerable today.

Reflection Question

- Where in your life is the enemy subtly trying to gain ground right now—and how can you respond with Scripture and deeper surrender?

Let's Pray Together

Heavenly Father,

Lead me away from every trap that distracts, deceives, or divides my heart from You. I surrender every hidden corner of my life, especially where I feel weak, vulnerable, or exhausted. Protect my spiritual house from pride, self-reliance, and false security.

Jesus, You overcame temptation in the wilderness. Help me resist temptation as You did—grounded in Your Word, surrendered in worship, and secure in the Father's love.

Holy Spirit, align my desires fully with Yours. Let this room of temptation become a place of truth, protection, and daily dependence.

Thank You that every temptation I face is already overcome through Jesus. Amen.

Where We Go from Here

Having resisted temptation by affirming our true identity and clinging to God's Word, we are now ready to enter the final room on the ground floor—the room of deliverance. There we will pray, "Deliver us from the evil one," and learn to walk in lasting freedom.

Take a deeper dive into this chapter by listening to this podcast episode:

https://ericcelerier.net/podcast-23

Are you ready to stand confidently in His victory?

Chapter 24

Deliver Us from Evil

"But deliver us from the evil one."

Matthew 6:13

We are in the final room on the ground floor of our house of prayer—where we also pray, "Deliver us from the evil one." This is not just a prayer for protection; it is a bold declaration of Christ's victory. It is the room where spiritual battles meet their resolution, where the power of heaven confronts the schemes of darkness. It is where the will of God, embraced in the previous room, becomes a shield of deliverance.

Facing the Reality of Evil

Have you ever faced situations that felt completely overwhelming—moments of fear, anxiety, or bitterness that seemed impossible to overcome? Evil isn't a distant concept. It is personal. It's the voice that tries to convince you that you are alone, unworthy, defeated. But the cross tells a different story.

When Jesus died on the cross, He didn't just suffer; He conquered. Paul declares:

> Having disarmed the powers and authorities, he made a public spectacle of them, triumphing over them by the cross. (Col. 2:15)

The cross is your guarantee that evil will never have the last word in your life.

The Power of Jesus' Victory

Years ago, I was scheduled to meet with a government official known for opposing Christian values. Friends warned me to be careful. But in prayer, I heard God whisper, "Look beyond her hostility. She needs Me." As I shared Christ's love, her eyes filled with tears. That day, I saw it clearly: evil cannot withstand the gentle, authoritative presence of Jesus.

Jesus doesn't just defeat evil—He delivers us daily.

Michael's breakthrough: "Bitterness toward a colleague nearly consumed me until I recognized it was evil in disguise. When I chose forgiveness, peace rushed in. Evil lost all power."

From Delivered to Deliverer

Jesus' victory isn't meant to stay within us—it's meant to flow through us. When the Ethiopian official received Christ (see Acts 8), his encounter led to spiritual transformation for an entire region. The Samaritan woman's story (see John 4) sparked revival in her village.

Your deliverance is not the end—it's the beginning of God's deliverance through you.

> He who is in you is greater than he who is in the world. (1 John 4:4 NKJV)

A Living Testimony

Deliverance extends far beyond your heart. Your house of prayer becomes a refuge—a place where others encounter the freedom of Christ. Through your prayers, families are restored, cities are impacted, and nations are healed.

Jesus' victory over evil is total. The final enemy—death—has been conquered. We now carry that victory into daily life, declaring with our lives, "Deliver us from the evil one," as we let light overcome darkness.

Three Steps to Daily Deliverance

1. **Recognize:** Identify evil's presence—fear, bitterness, temptation.
2. **Resist:** Declare God's truth boldly over your situation.
3. **Rely:** Trust fully in Christ's victory and presence within you.

Practical Steps to Walk in Victory

- **Immediate Declaration:** Say aloud, "Jesus has already defeated evil. I live today from His victory."
- **Visualize Protection:** Picture Jesus at the entrance of your spiritual house, guarding every room.

- **Share Your Deliverance:** Recall a moment when God set you free—and share it with someone who needs hope today.

Let's Pray Together

Father,

Thank You that Jesus has already conquered evil through the cross. Today I take refuge in that victory. Deliver me from every scheme of darkness trying to invade my heart, my family, or my calling.

Let my house of prayer be a stronghold of grace, protection, and mission—where Your light overcomes darkness and Your kingdom comes on earth as it is in heaven.

Fill me with Your Spirit. Let every prayer be a sword, every breath a declaration, every step a testimony to Your freedom.

In Jesus' victorious name, amen.

Lisa's freedom: "I lived captive to fear of rejection. Then I heard God whisper, 'Trust My love more than their opinions.' As I did, fear loosened its grip."

Where We Go from Here

Having taken refuge in the room of deliverance, we are now ready to anchor our entire house of prayer on its eternal foundation. In the next chapter, we'll boldly declare, "For Yours is the kingdom and the power and the glory forever."

Take a deeper dive into this chapter by listening to this podcast episode:

https://ericcelerier.net/podcast-24

Are you ready to ground your life in what lasts forever?

Reflection and Prayer

Reflection and Prayer

Part 5

THE CONNECTED HOUSE

Where Heaven Touches Earth through Prayer

Chapter 25

The Connected House of Prayer

We live in a world of highly connected homes. My own house is fully wired: sound systems, TVs, lights, air conditioning, security cameras—even the front door lock—are controllable from anywhere in the world. But when I speak about a "connected house," I mean something infinitely more impressive: the spiritual connection between the upper and lower levels of your house of prayer.

Each room on the upper level directly aligns with a corresponding room below, revealing a sacred symmetry woven into the Lord's Prayer. This design isn't random—it reflects God's deep desire to connect heaven and earth through prayer.

An Extraordinary Alignment

At the top of our spiritual house is the roof—"Our Father in heaven."

At the foundation lies our unshakable confidence—"For yours is the kingdom and the power and the glory forever."

These two truths hold everything together, anchoring our prayer life in God's eternal presence and purpose.

Now look at how each upper room aligns beautifully with a lower counterpart:

Upper Room 1: "Hallowed be your name"
Lower Room 1: "Give us today our daily bread"
As we honor His name, He provides for our needs—both spiritual and physical.

Upper Room 2: "Your kingdom come"
Lower Room 2: "Forgive us our debts, as we also have forgiven our debtors"
Forgiveness reveals the kingdom. It's not just personal—it's communal, reconciling and restoring what was broken.

Upper Room 3: "Your will be done, on earth as it is in heaven"
Lower Room 3: "Lead us not into temptation, but deliver us from the evil one"
Living in God's will guards our hearts from temptation and leads us into freedom.

This intentional alignment reveals a divine pattern: **Heaven leads. Earth follows.**

The Keys of Heaven and Earth

Jesus once said to Peter:

> I will give you the keys of the kingdom of heaven; whatever you bind on earth will be bound in heaven, and whatever you loose on earth will be loosed in heaven. (Matt. 16:19)

In Greek, the tense is even clearer: "will have been bound in heaven."

This means our prayers don't start something new—they **activate what God has already willed**.

Prayer is not persuasion. It is **partnership**.

> Julia said, "Praying Scripture aloud became like holding heaven's keys. As I declared God's Word, breakthrough came—earth aligned with heaven."

A Personal Story: My Car from Heaven

I'll never forget the day I discovered this truth.

I was a broke Bible student. Suddenly, I had no car—and I needed one urgently for ministry. Buying or renting was impossible. I felt helpless.

But instead of panicking, I boldly prayed. I declared God's promises. I believed that heaven had already moved.

A few days later, someone called unexpectedly and said, "Eric, I have something for you." When I arrived at his home, there was a car parked out front.

He smiled and said, "It's yours."

He had no idea I needed one. But heaven did.

Muriel and I were stunned. That car was already prepared above—**our prayer simply unlocked it here below.**

> Kayla affirmed, "Understanding my spiritual authority changed my life. When I pray with heaven, I help bring heaven to earth."

Practical Application

- **Speak Boldly:** Declare aloud one promise from Scripture. Let heaven's truth align your day.
- **Visualize Your Keys:** Imagine Jesus handing you the keys. As you pray, see yourself unlocking doors of provision, forgiveness, healing, and peace.
- **Encourage a Friend:** Share this principle with someone who needs it. Remind them: prayer opens what God has already prepared.

Spiritual Insight

Dallas Willard describes prayer as "talking to God about what we are doing together."[1]

It's not passive. It's not begging. It's divine partnership.

It's daily access to heaven's strategy, strength, and sufficiency.

Let's Pray Together

Heavenly Father,

Thank You for the sacred alignment between heaven and earth. Thank You for giving me the keys to Your kingdom.

Today, I step into bold, aligned prayer. I declare that heaven leads and I joyfully follow.

Let my house of prayer reflect Your design: provision, peace, purpose, and power flowing in every room.

Let me live connected—heart to heart, heaven to earth.

In Jesus' powerful name, amen.

Where We Go from Here

Now that we've discovered the sacred design of a connected house of prayer, we're ready for what comes next: the one who fills this house with breath, power, and presence—the Holy Spirit.

Are you ready to open every room to His transforming presence?

Take a deeper dive into this chapter by listening to this podcast episode:

https://ericcelerier.net/podcast-25

Chapter 26

The Spirit of the House

As we have seen, every room of our spiritual house is carefully connected to heaven's realities. But a connected house, no matter how beautifully designed, is empty without life. Now comes the most impactful moment: the house must be inhabited. The Spirit of God is not meant to visit occasionally—He longs to fill every space completely.

A connected house becomes truly alive only when filled with the Spirit who brings heaven's presence into every room. Sometimes, when entering a home, you immediately sense its spirit—whether welcoming and peaceful, or cold and unsettling. Beyond mere ambiance, what we experience is the spirit inhabiting that place. In your spiritual house of prayer, the presence that fills every room, breathes life into every prayer, and empowers every moment is meant to be none other than the Holy Spirit Himself.

The Promised Comforter

Jesus knew His disciples would face anxiety when He returned to the Father. So He gave them an extraordinary promise:

> I will ask the Father, and he will give you another advocate to help you and be with you forever—the Spirit of truth. (John 14:16–17)

The Holy Spirit isn't distant or abstract—He is God's personal, active presence within every believer. His arrival turns the ordinary into sacred spaces where heaven touches earth.

Pentecost: Heaven Invading Earth

After Jesus ascended, the disciples gathered in Jerusalem's upper room, waiting. Then, at Pentecost, heaven broke in:

> Suddenly a sound like the blowing of a violent wind came from heaven and filled the whole house. (Acts 2:2)

God's Spirit filled every corner, igniting hearts with boldness, joy, and spiritual gifts. The same Spirit who empowered Peter to preach with courage and clarity lives in you today.

As A. W. Tozer wrote:

> The Spirit-filled life is not a special, deluxe edition of Christianity. It is part and parcel of the total plan of God for His people.[1]

The Holy Spirit's Work in Your House of Prayer

- **He Guides:** "When he, the Spirit of truth, comes, he will guide you into all the truth." (John 16:13)

- **He Comforts:** As the "Advocate" (John 14:26) He brings peace and assurance.
- **He Empowers:** "You will receive power when the Holy Spirit comes on you." (Acts 1:8)
- **He Sanctifies:** The Spirit reveals hidden things, leading us into deeper repentance and transformation (see John 16:8).

Personal Reflection

How aware are you of the Holy Spirit's presence in your daily life? Are you inviting Him into every room?

I remember moments of deep discouragement in ministry. Turning to the Holy Spirit, even with a simple prayer, brought unexpected peace and surprising clarity. When we welcome Him, He transforms confusion into guidance, anxiety into worship.

Anna shared, "When I feel dry, the Holy Spirit revives my prayer life. His touch makes God's Word alive and personal."

Practical Application

- **Simple Invitation:** Right now, invite God's Spirit: "Holy Spirit, fill every room of my heart today."
- **Visualization:** Picture a mighty wind sweeping through your spiritual house, refreshing every room with God's peace, joy, and clarity.

- **Testimony:** Share a personal moment where the Spirit's presence brought peace or transformation. Encouragement multiplies faith!

Let's Pray Together

Holy Spirit,

Today we open every room of our hearts to You.

Fill our homes, our thoughts, and our lives. Ignite passion within us. Refresh what feels dry. Guide us into truth. Empower us to reflect Jesus boldly.

Make our spiritual houses places overflowing with Your joy, peace, and power.

In Jesus' mighty and precious name, amen.

Christopher witnessed, "One morning, praying quietly, the Spirit flooded me with a joy and hope I'd thought lost forever. Heaven truly invaded my heart."

Where We Go from Here

Having welcomed the Holy Spirit into every corner of our spiritual house, we now move joyfully to the foundations. In the next chapter, we will confidently declare: "Lord, everything—absolutely everything—belongs to You!"

Are you ready to explore the unshakable foundation of your house of prayer?

Take a deeper dive into this chapter by listening to this podcast episode:

https://ericcelerier.net/podcast-26

Chapter 27

Lord, Everything Belongs to You!

"For yours is the kingdom and the power and the glory forever."

Matthew 6:13

As we come to the foundations of our house of prayer, we are reminded of a life-changing truth: everything begins and ends with God.

When we started this journey, we noted that the doxology—"For yours is the kingdom and the power and the glory"—is not found in every ancient manuscript. Like the invisible foundations of a house, it might be overlooked by some. Yet it has always been essential, anchoring the entire spiritual structure.

Even though this line is absent in some gospel manuscripts, the early church quickly adopted it in worship, as attested by the *Didaché* (first century). Like solid footings hidden beneath the ground, this doxology supports the full weight of our prayers—even when unseen.

The roof is heaven. The rooms are our daily prayers. But the foundation—deep, unshakable—is this final declaration of God's eternal rule and unmatched authority.

Yours Is the Kingdom

"Kingdom"—from the Greek *basileia*—runs through every room of our spiritual house. God's kingdom is not fragile or fading; it is eternal and invincible.

King David declared it clearly:

> Yours, LORD, is the greatness and the power and the
> glory....
> Yours, LORD, is the kingdom;
> you are exalted as head over all. (1 Chron. 29:11)

When we declare "Yours is the kingdom," we step out of self-centered living and place our lives inside something far greater: God's reign. It reshapes our priorities, realigns our ambitions, and calls us to serve a higher purpose.

Yours Is the Power

The word "power" (*dunamis*) gives us the modern word "dynamite"—a symbol of explosive, transformative force.

Paul reminds us:

> Now to him who is able to do immeasurably more than all we ask or imagine, according to his power (*dunamis*) that is at work within us. (Eph. 3:20)

To say "Yours is the power" is to surrender our limitations and rely on divine strength. God's power doesn't merely support us—it works within us, turning impossible moments into testimonies.

> Colette reflected, "Recognizing that everything belongs to God transformed my mornings. Each new day became a miracle to celebrate."

Yours Is the Glory

Glory belongs to God alone. As Isaiah wrote:

> I am the LORD; that is my name!
> I will not yield my glory to another. (42:8)

Early in my ministry, God pressed this deeply into my heart: "Eric, whatever you accomplish, let the glory return to Me." That's why Psalm 115:1 became my daily reminder:

> Not to us, LORD, not to us
> but to your name be the glory.

Glory isn't about applause. It's about awe. It lifts our eyes from what we do to who God is.

Forever

This key word roots our lives in eternity:

> Your kingdom is an everlasting kingdom,
> and your dominion endures through all
> generations. (Ps. 145:13)

When we say "forever," we shift our perspective. We stop living for temporary outcomes and start living for eternal impact. It means letting today be shaped by heaven's tomorrow.

To live with eternity in mind is to build your house not on shifting sand but on the rock of God's unchanging reign.

Jocelyn added, "The more I acknowledge God's power and glory, the smaller my problems seem. Worship puts everything in the right perspective."

Practical Applications

- **Declaration:** Begin your prayers by saying, "Lord, everything belongs to You."
- **Visualization:** Picture your life resting on the strong foundations of His kingdom, His power, and His glory.
- **Shared Encouragement:** Keep a "Glory Journal" to document moments when God's kingdom, power, and glory shine through.

Let's Pray Together

Heavenly Father,

As I stand on the foundation of my house of prayer, I declare:

Yours is the kingdom. Yours is the power. Yours is the glory. Forever and ever.

Every breath I breathe, every step I take, every prayer I whisper—it all belongs to You. Anchor my heart in this eternal reality.

Teach me to live today as I will live forever—joyfully surrendered to Your glory.

In the mighty name of Jesus, amen.

Where We Go from Here

Now that our house of prayer stands fully established—rooted in God's kingdom, empowered by His Spirit, and crowned with His glory—we are ready for the final seal: the "amen."

This last word is not merely a conclusion. It is heaven's signature over your life.

Are you ready to declare it with boldness?

Take a deeper dive into this chapter by listening to this podcast episode:

https://ericcelerier.net/podcast-27

Chapter 28

AMEN—the Seal of Our Prayer

"Amen."

Matthew 6:13

This simple yet profound word concludes the Our Father, affirming that indeed the kingdom, the power, and the glory belong to God forever. The word "amen" (*ἀμήν* in Greek, *ןמֵאָ* in Hebrew) is much more than a polite closure to prayer—it is a declaration of unwavering faith and complete trust in God's promises.

Throughout our journey through the spiritual house of the Lord's Prayer, we have explored room after room, truth after truth, promise after promise. Now, with "amen," we firmly anchor our entire prayer, sealing it with assurance and trust.

The Meaning of "Amen"

"Amen" comes from the Hebrew root *ןמא* (*a-m-n*), meaning "firm, reliable, and trustworthy." It signifies truthfulness and certainty, affirming that what we have spoken aligns perfectly with God's eternal truth and faithfulness. Each time we say "amen," we are confidently declaring, "It is true, and it shall come to pass."

In the Old Testament, "amen" often marked the conclusion of prayers, blessings, and covenantal agreements, indicating the people's agreement and faith. When we say "amen," we join generations of believers affirming God's faithfulness across history.

Patrick shared, "For me, praying in the name of Jesus is affirming my complete trust in God's promises. Saying 'amen' isn't routine anymore—it's my declaration that Jesus is reliable and faithful."

Jesus Himself Is the "Amen"

Yet in Jesus, "amen" takes on an even deeper, richer meaning. Jesus frequently used "amen"—over a hundred times in the Gospels—to emphasize weighty truths, often saying, "Truly, truly [amen, amen], I say to you ..."

Even more meaningfully, Jesus reveals Himself as the living embodiment of "amen":

> These are the words of the Amen, the faithful and true witness, the ruler of God's creation. (Rev. 3:14)

Jesus doesn't merely say "amen"—He *is* the Amen. He is the firm foundation upon which every promise of God stands secure and fulfilled. As the apostle Paul declares:

> No matter how many promises God has made, they are "Yes" in Christ. And so through him the "Amen" is spoken by us to the glory of God. (2 Cor. 1:20)

Praying in the Name of Jesus

When we conclude our prayers with "amen," we affirm that our requests, praises, and declarations are sealed in Christ. "Amen" becomes a joyful cry of certainty:

- Amen—God is my Father and loves me infinitely!
- Amen—God's name is honored!
- Amen—God's kingdom is coming!
- Amen—God's will is accomplished!
- Amen—We are daily provided for!
- Amen—We are forgiven and forgiving!
- Amen—We are led away from temptation!
- Amen—We are delivered from evil!
- Amen—All glory belongs to God forever!
- Amen—Jesus reigns forever!

Practical Application: Living "Amen"

- **Immediate Action:** As you finish any prayer today, pause and declare "amen," consciously aligning yourself with Jesus, the faithful witness guaranteeing your prayer.
- **Reflection:** Visualize Jesus standing beside you, personally affirming every request you present

to the Father, strengthening your heart with His faithful assurance.

- **Faith Practice:** Throughout the day, whisper "amen" in your heart whenever you face a situation needing trust. Let it anchor your spirit in Christ's reliability.

Benjamin shared, "My understanding of 'amen' completely changed when I realized it represents Jesus. Now each 'amen' I speak is an act of worship and surrender, trusting Jesus entirely."

Let's Pray Together

Heavenly Father,

Today, as we conclude our prayers with "amen," we boldly affirm that all Your promises are trustworthy and true. Thank You for giving us Jesus—the faithful and true Amen—in whom every promise finds its perfect fulfillment.

Strengthen our faith to trust You wholeheartedly. Help us to pray boldly, confidently knowing You hear and answer us according to Your perfect will.

In the mighty, faithful, and powerful name of Jesus, our eternal Amen, we pray.

Amen.

Where We Go from Here

As we seal this journey through the house of prayer with the mighty Amen of Jesus Himself, we now prepare for the greatest adventure: to live the Our Father prayer in every breath, every step, and every moment.

Take a deeper dive into this chapter by listening to this podcast episode: **https://ericcelerier.net/podcast-28**

Our next step is not just about praying words—it's about **carrying God's presence into every aspect of life**.

Before we move forward, let me share with you a real-life story—one that perfectly captures the transforming power of prayer when heaven truly meets earth.

A True Story: When Heaven Stepped In

Before we step into the final part of our journey—"Living as a House of Prayer"—let's pause.

You've now explored the deep meaning behind every word of the Lord's Prayer. You've walked through every room, from rooftop to foundation. You've seen how heaven meets earth—and how your heart becomes the sacred meeting place.

Now it's time to move from **understanding** to **embodying**. From praying the prayer to living it.

But before we do, let me share a true and remarkable story. A testimony that reminds us with unmistakable clarity: when we dare to pray with faith, **heaven truly touches earth**.

The Prayer That Carried Him

This story is real (only the name has been changed for confidentiality). I know the man personally.

Patrick, a CEO of a major food company in a nation plagued by corruption, was respected for his faith and unwavering integrity. But one day, he discovered he had become the target of a political vendetta. A fabricated arrest warrant was issued, and danger closed in quickly.

In a desperate bid at escape, Patrick hid inside the trunk of a car. The journey was agonizing. Not only was it stifling hot, but every bump sent waves of pain through his back—already weakened by years of spinal damage that normally required a rigid brace.

But in that dark, airless place, Patrick did something powerful: he prayed the Our Father.

Over and over again, he whispered it. The trunk became more than a hiding place; it became a sanctuary, a house of prayer.

Hours later, he emerged safely ... and miraculously healed. The chronic pain that had plagued him for years was gone.

Still in danger, he boarded a small boat under the cover of darkness. Halfway across the waters, the engine died. No light. No fuel. No hope.

Again, Patrick prayed: "Our Father ..."

Against all odds, help came. The boat reached safety.

Yet the trial wasn't over. Back home, Patrick was arrested and brought before a judge. A prison sentence seemed inevitable. But even there, Patrick whispered again, "Thy will be done."

Then came the miracle.

The president of the nation himself intervened—personally contacting the minister of justice. Hours later, Patrick was released and walked freely into the arms of his wife.

That night, lying beside her, he wept with gratitude. What once seemed ordinary—sleeping at home—had become a sacred miracle. He repeated the Our Father over and over again, tears streaming down his face.

He knew now, more than ever, that **to God belong the kingdom, the power, and the glory forever**.

Today, Patrick still faces challenges—but he lives in deep peace. He prays the Lord's Prayer daily—not out of ritual but as an actual living connection to the God who saves, who speaks, and who moves.

His story brings to mind the words of Job:

> I know that my redeemer lives,
> and that in the end he will stand on the earth.
> (19:25)

Where We Go from Here: Living as a House of Prayer

Now that we've prayed the Lord's Prayer from rooftop to foundation, we are invited into something even greater:

To become the house.

In the next part, you'll learn how to carry this prayer not just in your mouth but in every breath ... not just in church but in every corner of your life.

Welcome to part 6: "Living as a House of Prayer"—a daily, dynamic life where God's presence flows through you, blessing the world around you.

Are you ready to live it?

Reflection and Prayer

Reflection and Prayer

Part 6

LIVING AS A HOUSE OF PRAYER

Chapter 29

A Practical Guide for Daily Prayer

Throughout this journey, you've walked through the rich, life-giving rooms of your spiritual house of prayer, stepping through each phrase of the Our Father.

But how can you now live out these truths in your daily rhythm?

Here is a simple, flexible guide to help you inhabit the Lord's Prayer daily—making it a continual source of life, connection, and transformation.

Reminder: The Ten Parts of the Our Father House

Before diving into the methods, let's remember the structure of your spiritual house:

- "Our Father in heaven"—the roof
- "Hallowed be your name"—room 1 upstairs
- "Your kingdom come"—room 2 upstairs

- "Your will be done"—room 3 upstairs
- "On earth as it is in heaven"—the staircase linking heaven and earth
- "Give us today our daily bread"—room 1 downstairs
- "And forgive us our debts, as we also have forgiven our debtors"—room 2 downstairs
- "And lead us not into temptation"—room 3 downstairs
- "But deliver us from the evil one"—still room 3 downstairs
- "For yours is the kingdom and the power and the glory forever. Amen."—the foundations

Each part is a living space you can enter daily, nurturing your communion with God.

Method 1: The Meditative Walk

This method inspired this book.

Go for a peaceful walk—whether in nature or in your neighborhood—praying the Lord's Prayer phrase by phrase.

With every few steps, visualize yourself entering a new room of your spiritual house. Let the rhythm of walking and praying align your heart with God's heartbeat.

Method 2: Breathing the Lord's Prayer

This is inspired by ancient Jewish tradition, where even the sacred name YHWH was seen as the sound of breath:

YH—inhale
WH—exhale

From the first breath of a newborn to the gentle sigh of rest, our lives echo His name.

How to Practice:

- Find a quiet space.
- Inhale slowly and pray the beginning: "Our Father in heaven ..."
- Exhale gently and rest in His presence.
- Continue phrase by phrase, letting your breath carry the prayer.

Breathing the Our Father allows your body, mind, and spirit to become a living prayer.

Method 3: Prayerful Repetition

Repeating the Lord's Prayer slowly is impactful. It's not vain repetition—it's embedding truth.

How to Practice:

- Pray slowly and attentively.
- Pause when a phrase speaks to you.
- Let the Holy Spirit reveal new meaning.

Method 4: Phrase of the Day

Choose one phrase to carry throughout your day.

How to Practice:

- Write it somewhere visible—your phone, mirror, or journal.
- Let it guide your thoughts, reactions, and prayers.

Method 5: Community Prayer

Remember, Jesus taught us to say "our" Father.

How to Practice:

- Pray slowly with family, friends, or your church group.
- Reflect together on how it becomes real in your lives.

Method 6: Embodied Prayer with Gestures

Engage your whole being—body, mind, and spirit.

How to Practice:

- "Our Father in heaven": Raise hands overhead.
- "Hallowed be your name": Stretch arms upward.
- "Your kingdom come": Reach forward.
- "Your will be done": Open hands in surrender.
- "On earth as it is in heaven": Form a circle with your arms.
- "Give us today our daily bread": Lift open palms.
- "Forgive us our debts": Cross arms over your heart.
- "As we also have forgiven our debtors": Extend one hand outward in release.

- "Lead us not into temptation": Push palms outward.
- "Deliver us from the evil one": Lower arms with strength.
- "For yours is the kingdom": Lift arms in praise.
- "Amen": Raise hands in humble worship.

Method 7: Create Your Own Prayer Pathway

Let creativity flourish—paint, dance, sing, sculpt, or journal through the Lord's Prayer.

One woman designed a prayer garden in her backyard, each plant representing a phrase of the Lord's Prayer.

Let the Spirit guide you.

How to Practice:

- Choose one pathway from above and live it today.
- Keep a prayer journal to record insights.
- Share with a trusted friend or group to encourage one another.

Let's Pray Together

Heavenly Father,

Thank You for building within me a house of prayer.

Help me walk through its rooms daily with reverence, joy, and expectancy. Fill my prayers with Your Spirit, my steps with Your presence, and my heart with Your love.

Let my life reflect Your kingdom, Your power, and Your glory.

In Jesus' name, amen.

Where We Go from Here

Take a deeper dive into this chapter by listening to this podcast episode:
https://ericcelerier.net/podcast-29

You've walked through every room of the house of prayer. You've breathed its air, climbed its stairs, stood in its glory. Prayer is not only communication—it is communion. Not only asking—but becoming.

You are now the house where the Father dwells, the Son is honored, and the Spirit moves.

But this journey isn't over. The Lord's Prayer was never meant to stay in the quiet corners of devotion. It's meant to overflow. Into your relationships, your work, your creativity, your compassion.

You are now a carrier of God's presence. A living house of prayer.

And now, let's take one final step together—toward becoming that house of prayer in the world, every day, in every way.

Let's turn the page.

Chapter 30

Conclusion—Living as a House of Prayer

Congratulations! You have completed a remarkable spiritual journey through the house of the Our Father. But this is not an ending—it's a beginning. The beginning of living every day more intentionally, more fully, and more joyfully as a house of prayer.

Throughout this journey, we've discovered that prayer is not merely something we do—it's the sacred space where heaven and earth meet within us. Every phrase of the Lord's Prayer is a room built for encounter. And now, you are invited to dwell there—not occasionally, but always.

Walking through Your House of Prayer

Let's take one more walk through your spiritual house:

- **The Roof** ("Our Father in heaven"): You live under the shelter of perfect love.

- **The Room of Sanctification** ("Hallowed be your name"): Your life honors God in thought, word, and action.
- **The Kingdom Room** ("Your kingdom come"): You carry His kingdom wherever you go.
- **The Will Room** ("Your will be done"): You choose obedience and trust over control.
- **The Staircase of Grace** ("On earth as it is in heaven"): You walk the living bridge where heaven touches earth.
- **The Bread Room** ("Give us today our daily bread"): You receive fresh nourishment—spirit, soul, and body.
- **The Forgiveness Room** ("Forgive us our debts"): You breathe the atmosphere of grace and reconciliation.
- **The Room of Protection** ("Lead us not into temptation, but deliver us from the evil one"): You stand firm in Christ's victory.
- **The Foundations** ("For yours is the kingdom and the power and the glory"): You anchor your entire life on God's eternal strength.
- **The Amen**: You affirm with every breath that Jesus is the yes and amen to every promise.

You are not just visiting a house of prayer. You *are* the house. A living temple. A sacred place where God's presence dwells and where others can encounter Him through you.

Practical Ways to Deepen Your Daily Prayer Life

- **Begin Intentionally:** Each morning, step consciously into your spiritual house—even if just for a moment.
- **Journal Your Journey:** Write down how God meets you room by room. Track your growth, struggles, and breakthroughs.
- **Forgive Quickly:** Don't let bitterness take root. Let no offense build walls in your house.
- **Share and Encourage:** Invite others into this journey. Build a neighborhood of houses of prayer.

Where We Go From Here

You are now a living house of prayer. Carry this house into your workplace, your family, your friendships. Let heaven flow through you into earth, step by step, breath by breath.

And remember: You are not alone. Every time you say "Our Father," you join millions around the world—believers who are, like you, becoming places where heaven and earth connect.

A Final Word of Encouragement

The notable preacher Leonard Ravenhill is credited with this insight:

> A man who is intimate with God will never be intimidated by men.

Walk in that intimacy. Live in that boldness. Let prayer be not just what you say—but who you are.

Let's Pray Together

Heavenly Father,

As I close this journey through the Lord's Prayer, I open a new chapter of life—walking with You daily, carrying Your presence into every moment.

Make my life a vibrant house of prayer: a place where Your name is honored, where Your kingdom advances, where Your will is embraced with joy.

Take a deeper dive into this chapter by listening to this podcast episode:

https://ericcelerier.net/podcast-30

Feed me daily with Your living bread. Forgive me, and help me forgive. Strengthen me against temptation. Deliver me from every evil.

Today, I dedicate myself again to You. Let my every thought, word, and action reflect Your kingdom, Your power, and Your glory—now and forever.

In Jesus' faithful, victorious name—our eternal Amen—I pray, amen.

Friend, This Is Just the Beginning

You are a house of prayer. A living gateway between heaven and earth.

Go forth. Carry His presence into every space. Let His light shine through you.

The world is waiting. Heaven is ready. And God is with you.

With heartfelt affection
and unshakable faith,
Your friend and brother,
Eric Célérier

Reflection and Prayer

Reflection and Prayer

The Community of Prayer Carriers

You've completed the final chapter … but the journey continues.

Around the world, thousands are walking with you—becoming living houses of prayer, carrying God's presence into every area of life.

This book has helped you build your own spiritual house. Now it's time to open the doors, let the light shine, and join a global family of faith.

These believers, just like you, have experienced transformation. Their stories—simple, sincere, and sacred—show us what happens when the Lord's Prayer is not only prayed but lived.

If God is doing it in them, He is surely doing it in you too. Welcome to the family.

Reader Stories of Transformation

"Previously, I understood that as a Christian, I was part of God's spiritual family. But discovering that I myself am meant to be a living house of prayer transformed my faith completely! Now, prayer feels deeply personal yet connected to the whole church."

—Diane

"As a Catholic, I recited the Lord's Prayer regularly during Mass, but it often felt routine. Through this journey, each phrase came alive. Prayer is now a real conversation with my Father—personal and strengthening."

—Pamela

"What moved me most was the phrase 'on earth as it is in heaven.' It became a daily cry for transformation—not only in my life but in the world around me."

—Frances

"*Becoming a House of Prayer* has been the best spiritual book I've read this year! I've already gifted it to three friends. It helped me rediscover the Lord's Prayer and worship with deeper passion."

—Kimberly

"Every phrase of the Lord's Prayer feels like a direct encounter with Jesus now. My times of worship have never felt more real."

—Anne

"I've always prayed 'Your will be done.' But now it means something deeper—daily surrender. This book taught me how."

—Jodi

"Now, every word of the Lord's Prayer echoes in my heart. It has strengthened my faith and enriched my closest relationships."

—Julia

"My house of prayer is no longer a dream—it's a living space of peace. Thank you for opening my eyes."

—Theresa

"This journey was an answer to prayer. At first, I felt lost. Now, I feel deeply connected—to Jesus, to His words, and to His people."

—Julie

"These chapters changed me. Becoming a house of prayer wasn't just a metaphor—it became my reality. What a sacred adventure!"

—Natalie

"As a single mom, I was overwhelmed. But now, with my daughters, we pray the Lord's Prayer together—and God feels so close."

—Patricia

"Even after years in the church, I felt spiritually distant. This book opened every room in my heart to God again."

—Phil

"I've been a believer for decades, but now for the first time, I understand what it means to be a house of prayer. I'll never pray the same way again."

—Norman

"My prayers are no longer vague. Now they're clear, humble, and connected—full of respect, dependence, and intimacy."

—Sebastian

"From the first chapter to the final 'amen,' I saw Jesus more clearly. Now I pray with joy, confidence, and expectation."

—Faith

What About You?

Now it's your turn.

Just as you were invited earlier to draw your house of prayer or write your reflections, you are now invited to testify.

What has God done in you through this journey?

Write it. Share it. Let your story open doors for someone else.

You are no longer just reading—you're carrying His presence.

Notes

Chapter 2

1. Timothy Keller, *Prayer: Experiencing Awe and Intimacy with God* (New York: Viking, 2016), 80.

Chapter 3

1. "5045.tekton," Strong's Lexicon, Bible Hub, accessed April 28, 2025, https://biblehub.com/greek/5045.htm.

2. Greg Leith, CONVENE Leadership Summit (Newport Beach, California), April 23, 2015.

3. See also Ephesians 2:10 in the New Living Translation.

4. C. S. Lewis, *Mere Christianity* (New York: Touchstone, 1996), 176.

Chapter 4

1. John Ortberg, *The Life You've Always Wanted* (Grand Rapids, MI: Zondervan, 2002), chap. 1.

Chapter 7

1. Albert Einstein, "The World As I See It," *Forum and Century*, vol. 84 (1931), 193–94.

2. Timothy Keller, *Prayer: Experiencing Awe and Intimacy with God* (New York: Penguin, 2016), 80.

3. "3466.mustērion," Strong's Lexicon, Bible Hub, https://biblehub.com/greek/3466.htm.

Chapter 10

1. Paul David Tripp, *Instruments in the Redeemer's Hands: People in Need of Change Helping People in Need of Change* (Phillipsburg, NJ: P&R, 2002), 116.

Chapter 18

1. This last sentence of the Lord's Prayer is found in the footnote of the NIV and most other translations.

2. C. S. Lewis, *Mere Christianity* (San Francisco: Harper, 2025), 78.

Chapter 19

1. Max Lucado, *Just Like Jesus: A Heart like His* (Thomas Nelson, 2012), 8.

Chapter 20

1. Dallas Willard, "Live Life to the Full," Dallas Willard Ministries, April 14, 2001, https://dwillard.org/resources/articles/live-life-to-the-full.

Chapter 21

1. "Origen on Prayer," (Grand Rapids, MI: Christian Classics Ethereal Library), accessed May 21, 2025, www.ccel.org/ccel/o/origen/prayer/cache/prayer.pdf.

Chapter 25

1. Dallas Willard, *The Divine Conspiracy: Jesus' Master Class for Life* (Grand Rapids, MI: HarperChristian Resources), 71.

Chapter 26

1. A. W. Tozer, *How to Be Filled with the Holy Spirit* (Christian Publications, 1960).